# MONEY
# GAMES

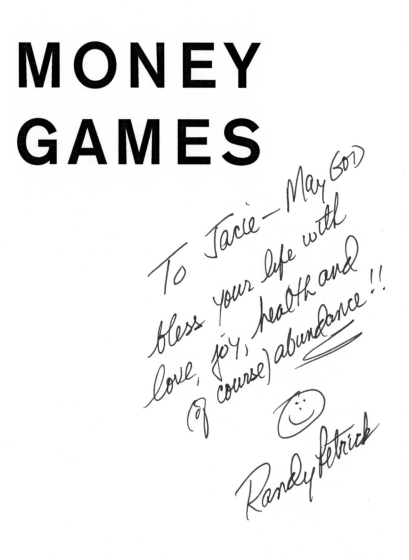

To Jacie — May God
bless your life with
love, joy, health and
(of course) abundance!!

Randy Petrick

# MONEY GAMES

## 85 Fun Ways to Save Money and Attract Abundance

RANDY PETRICK

iUniverse, Inc.
New York Bloomington Shanghai

**Money Games**
**85 Fun Ways to Save Money and Attract Abundance**

Copyright © 2008 by Randy Petrick

iUniverse books may be ordered through booksellers or by contacting:

iUniverse
1663 Liberty Drive
Bloomington, IN 47403
www.iuniverse.com
1-800-Authors (1-800-288-4677)

Because of the dynamic nature of the Internet, any Web addresses or links contained in this book may have changed since publication and may no longer be valid.

The information, ideas, and suggestions in this book are not intended to render professional advice. Before following any suggestions contained in this book, you should consult your personal accountant or other financial advisor. Neither the author nor the publisher shall be liable or responsible for any loss or damage allegedly arising as a consequence of your use or application of any information or suggestions in this book.

ISBN: 978-0-595-48197-2 (pbk)
ISBN: 978-0-595-71907-5 (cloth)
ISBN: 978-0-595-60289-6 (ebk)

Printed in the United States of America

## WHAT IS YOUR FINANCIAL SITUATION?

- Are you discouraged and up to your eyeballs in debt?
- Are doubt and despair your constant financial companions?
- Do you have trouble saving more than a nickel before an emergency hits?
- Do you continually run out of money before the end of the month?
- Do you want to get out from under those lousy bills?

## HAVE YOU BEEN SEARCHING FOR …

- … a financial book that is humorous and fun to read?
- … an author who isn't afraid to whack you upside the head when you misbehave?
- … a book full of genuinely workable ideas to help you escape from debt and despair?

## YOUR CHANCE TO BREAK FREE HAS ARRIVED!

- Have fun and save money like never before!
- Dramatically change your financial life for the better!
- Say yes to abundance!

If you've never been able to save money successfully, then your time is now, and this book has the answers you need.

## THE TOOLS ARE IN YOUR HANDS. LET THE GAMES BEGIN!

*To Gwyn, the loveliest inspiration an author could ever ask for*

# Contents

*Introduction*      *1*

   *What This Book Is*     *1*

   *What This Book Isn't*     *3*

   *How This Book Is Arranged*     *3*

   *Where to Find the Answers to the "Vital" Money Questions*     *4*

## Adventure Games

Restaurant Roulette     9
*Eat well; get rich?*

"Strip" Poker     10
*A fun way to get your friends to pay for your meals.*

## Bedtime Games

Making Money while You Sleep     13
*Let your money work 24/7 so you don't have to.*

Pillow Talk     14
*How to talk to yourself just after you close your eyes for the night.*

## Bored Games

Cheap-Show Movies     19
*It's the same movie! (And it's still dark in here.)*

Go Fish     20
*One pole, two boots, and say hello to Bob.*

Makin' Whoopee     21
*A retirement "quickie."*

## "Card" Games

AAA      25
*One card, free stuff, and lots of discounts.*

Go Fish II      27
*Cross the "bridge" with lots of "hearts" and you'll be in "spades."*

Let's Make a Deal!      28
*The best invention since electricity—and it's worse than a tornado.*

The Discover Game      30
*How to make money with plastic.*

## Computer and Spy Games

Browsing Around      35
*Gain some sense, save some cents.*

CEO/I Spy      38
*Pretend you are with the FBI or CIA.*

The GEEK Game      40
*It's a game where the family geek becomes the family hero!*

## Critter Games

Charlie Bird      45
*You might want to go take a shower before reading about this game; you are about to "come clean."*

Duck, Duck, Goose      47
*If you get one of these in the mail, you'd better duck, or you'll be the goose.*

Horse Poo      50
*It's a really "stable" game.*

Hummingbird      51
*Friendly fun with furiously flapping, feathered fowl!*

Pig      54
*Don't go getting your hogback up. Just get the pig out.*

Raptor      56
*It might as well be called "Cannibal," because someone wants you for dinner.*

## Family Games

Appreciation      61
*Enjoying FREE-dom.*

The Garden Hose Game      62
*The whole family can play, but beware … it's a little kinky.*

Twins      64
*It must be like eating sawdust with lumps.*

## Geographical Games

Euphrates      69
*Toss me in. I'll find the pearl!*

Mississippi (MSI-MSI-YIPPEE)      70
*It's about Saint Bernards and garden hoses.*

## Magical Games

Hocus-Focus      75
*Control your actions; change your results.*

Negotiation      78
*Are you ready for the seven magic words?*

Stardust      80
*The "Big Bang" and the Magic Kingdom.*

The Magic Box      83
*Having one can completely transform your financial life.*

Time Travel      86
*H. G. Wells will be jealous!*

## Musical Games

Fanfare       91
*Programming your brain for success.*

Trombone       93
*You'll want some very dark sunglasses—this one's outrageous!*

## Quick Hit Games

Another Dam(n) Game       97
*Put a giant smile on your face. You'll be living large!*

Barbecue       99
*Fifteen minutes a day is all I ask.*

Chimes ("Smelling" Your Way to Success)       100
*It starts innocently on the patio, but then it starts getting smelly.*

Composting       102
*Some rottin' advice.*

Generator/Alternator       104
*It's a powerful question to help you generate better alternatives and make better choices.*

RASKLE       106
*How recognizing the sound of a "skooch" and listening to thunder can make you millions.*

Shopping       108
*You have my permission to quote me on this.*

Sunshine on Your Shoulder       110
*All I really wanted was a nap!*

Write On!       112
*It's true—the first year really felt pitiful.*

# Savings Games

10-10-10                                                           117
*Poor people spend first and save what's left. Rich people ...*

Breathing                                                          119
*At least I admit it when I'm odd.*

Daily Double                                                       121
*... and me without a coupon in sight.*

Double Daily Double                                                123
*I wish I had a dollar for every time I made one of these mistakes ...*

Escalator                                                          125
*They're not fast, but they're always moving.*

Fast and Furious                                                   126
*Here are fourteen things to do if your present financial condition is pretty pitiful,
or at least somewhere less than optimal.*

For Better or for Worse                                            128
*There are two roads here ...*

Fortune Teller                                                     130
*One word makes a world of difference.*

Free Money                                                         132
*Nothing beats the feeling of putting one over on the uncle.*

Fund-a-mentals                                                     135
*Failing to plan is a common reason that many people experience financial
disaster.*

Half and Half                                                      137
*Finding the fastest way to reduce your financial stress.*

HOK and GOK (a.k.a. "Meet Mr. Murphy")                             139
*It may rain on your parade someday.*

Just Desserts                                                      141
*Dramatically reduce your restaurant bills while still having fun.*

Machine Gun                                                        143
*If your finances are wounded and your debt is killing you, start here first.*

Mostly Old Numbers 146
*If you spend the money now, it's gone.*

New Numbers 148
*The game for anyone who's ever said "God, give me patience ... and give it to me **now,** please!"*

Pajama Party 149
*Put your passbook in pj's, but never let it sleep at home.*

Pajama Party, Version II 151
*It's all about learning how to have happy money.*

Pennies from Heaven 153
*But what if the penny is upside down?*

Piece of Mine 155
*Sharing is a wonderful privilege, not a duty. Just don't give the house away.*

Pine Mountain Ragtime 158
*Can you spell "VROOOM?"*

Piranha 161
*"Do you really want to put your hand in there?"*

Recliner 163
*Is eighteen years long enough?*

"That Guy's" Game 165
*A game so good you'll need to be wary.*

Uncle Wiggly 166
*Don't leave your money on this uncle's table.*

What's in Your Pocket(book)? 167
*The one game neurotics always win.*

Wheels of Fortune 169
*Driving like a millionaire.*

Where's the Beef? 171
*It's not yoga, but you'll love to bend and stretch.*

## Thinking Games

Opsticles 175
*No matter how dire your circumstances ...*

Pelican 178
*At least I recognize my neuroses ... and I'm sure my new medications will help.*

The "I" Exam 180
*How to make your own diagnosis, plan your treatment, and get better.*

## The Weather Game

Winter 185
*Getting your "donkey" out of Dodge before the snow flies.*

## The "No-No" Games

Bondage 191
*Are you jealous of the neighbor with the nicer house, the nicer car, and the bigger swimming pool? Here's how to get the sweetest revenge.*

Bric-a-Brac and Beyond 193
*How did we get from mix-it-yourself, frozen orange juice to certified organic, 100 percent pure pomegranate juice and homemade smoothies?*

Holiday 198
*Thank goodness you have plastic. If you were carrying cash, you'd have to go back to the bank.*

L.A. Story 202
*And why the heck don't you do something about those nasty wrinkles around your eyes?*

Lemmings 205
*Are you in line, following along?*

Lemmings II (Also Known as "Gossip") 207
*Where are you getting your financial advice?*

Monopoly (Diversification, Part I)    209
*You have the best chance of staying afloat if you have several different life rafts available.*

Speeding (Diversification, Part II)    211
*Speed limits change from place to place and time to time, and your investments need to do the same.*

The "Albuquerque Low"    215
*A long, unexpected drive at midnight was the consequence of our failure to plan.*

The Sin of the Desert    217
*Truly wealthy people are generally the most giving, sharing, and open people you will ever meet.*

Yacht-Sea    219
*First you have to have somewhere to keep the darn thing.*

## The Final Game!

The Antithesis Game    223
*Live life, love everybody, and **spend** your money!*

*Golden Nuggets*    *225*
*The Top TEN Financial "Golden Nuggets"*    *225*

*References*    *229*

# Introduction

## What This Book Is

If you are not fabulously wealthy but would like to get a lot closer to that financial position—and have fun in the process—then this book is for you.[1]

The premise of this book is that it is possible for almost anyone to acquire significant assets. I know—I've proven it. At age twenty-five, I had a net worth of $1,500 (consisting mainly of an old, beaten-up Volvo) and an income of $11,000 per year. My savings and investments amounted to a grand total of $50 a month. But now, twenty-eight years later, I'm rapidly approaching multimillionaire status.

What happened? That's the story of this book. The first thing you need to know is that I'm no financial genius. I'm not a day trader or a real estate tycoon, and I haven't inherited great wealth. I made my money a few dollars at a time, and so can you. Whatever your current age or financial status, you can completely transform your finances and become a wealthy person as if by magic.

What's the secret? Saving and investing money has to be fun! If something isn't fun, I won't do it. Therefore, throughout the last twenty-five years, I've looked for every possible fun way to save money. That's what this book is about—sharing those ideas with you so that you also can have fun and build your wealth at the same time.

Is it easy? It is, and it isn't. Is it easy to play these "games," have fun, and save lots of money? Yes, it absolutely is. Is it easy to stay disciplined, keep holding onto your money, and let it grow when the numbers start getting large? Sometimes it isn't.

We live in a consumer society, and having $100,000 or $200,000 saved up can make for some nice temptations. Just think what you could do with that much money—travel the world, buy a Ferrari, buy a yacht, or buy a thousand pairs of shoes!

The truth is, attaining wealth involves discipline as well as fun. However, as you watch your net worth start to grow and grow and grow, saving becomes something you *want* to do rather than something you *have* to do.

---

[1] If you happen to be Warren Buffet, Bill Gates, or Donald Trump, you may be tempted to put this book back on the shelf. Instead, perhaps you'd like to buy copies to donate to all the libraries in the United States. As of 2004, there were 9,210 public libraries, in case you were wondering.

1

If you could see a graph of how my wife's and my net worth has grown, you would notice that in the beginning, that growth was painfully slow and seemed to be going nowhere. (We had a whopping $600 at the end of the first year of saving!) However, with time and patience and perseverance, what eventually happened was nothing short of remarkable. We have been magnificently rewarded for the discipline we had in our early years.

Like most people, my wife and I started out believing that spending was fun and saving was—yes, let's come right out and say it—boring! Did that change? Yes. We discovered that saving, investing, and having lots of fun aren't mutually exclusive. It really is possible to spend money, save money, and (surprise!) still have a blast as you go through life.

Imagine taking $600 and multiplying it by three thousand. That equals $1.8 million dollars—and that's what happened to our $600 over the course of twenty-seven years as we used the ideas you'll find in this book.[2] How many dollars do you think you could save today if you knew that every single one of them would be worth $3,000 later? You'd think twice about that Starbucks coffee you are about to buy, wouldn't you? And that is exactly my point.

Would it be more fun to spend all your money today or to have a lot more to spend later? You could argue for spending it today, I suppose. However, if you could save a dollar today and watch it grow into $3,000 in the future, something tells me that future money may be even more enjoyable than today's dollar.

When the money you've saved starts making money for you—and it will—that's when you'll start walking around with a grin on your face that will leave people wondering what you've been up to.

One of my favorite things is going to sleep at night knowing that even though I've stopped working for the day, my money is still silently working away for me and growing by itself all through the night. I know that when I wake up, I'll be richer than I was when I went to sleep. That's worth smiling about!

The first year that our investments made more money than I made from my job is a year I'll never forget. That was one exciting experience, and it's one you can have too. Take a moment right now and imagine the giant smile on your face when that happens to you! (Go ahead, try a practice grin—no one's watching!) If you start taking action today and keep taking action, you will experience that joy one day, just as we did.

---

[2]   Yes, I did say twenty-seven years! Building wealth happens slowly at the beginning, but happily, the pace increases rapidly later on. It took us nineteen years to build an initial net worth equal to the amount that our net worth *increased* last year! Don't give up just because the pace initially seems slow.

Your task is simple: browse this book, find the games that appeal to you, and try them out. You will be excited to see just how easy it is to build wealth and have fun at the same time.

## What This Book Isn't

Before we get started, you also need to know what this book isn't. This book will not teach you the secrets of Wall Street, how to buy real estate with nothing down, or how to make 160 percent per year on your investments. This is not a book full of magical secrets that will let you go from having zero net worth this year to being a millionaire next year. It's worth saying again: you will not get rich overnight.

This is also not a book filled with specific investment advice. There are already plenty of books out there to help you invest the money you save. (See References for a good starter list and go to www.wordsofabundance.com for additional information.) You will find some broad, general advice here, but for specifics on investing, you'll want to dig deeper elsewhere.

But in order to dig deeper, you must have a shovel—that is, you must start gaining some ground and accumulating some cash to invest. If you read no further than this page, at least learn this secret: successful savers start saving and keep on saving. Saving is the shovel that starts the process.

Are you deeply in debt? As the saying goes, "If you find yourself in a hole, the first thing to do is stop digging." Use your shovel to move the dirt in a positive direction! Start slowly adding dirt to the bottom of the hole, and you will soon find yourself at ground level. Keep adding dirt, and you can eventually have a giant mound as big as the pyramids of Egypt.

Slow (or stop) your spending, start saving, and keep on saving. That's the only secret to attaining great wealth. Can it really be that simple? Yes, but simple doesn't always mean easy. It only becomes easy when you add *fun* to the equation. That's what this book will help you do.

## How This Book Is Arranged

All the money-saving games are arranged in alphabetical order and by type of game. There are adventure games, bedtime games, card games, family games, travel games, and many more.

You will see some overlap between some of the games. Money games are a little like scrambled eggs. Even though the basic dish is made with plain old eggs, people make it differently by adding other ingredients. I have seen scrambled eggs made with salt, pepper, cheese, onions, ketchup, Tabasco, mushrooms, potatoes, shrimp … We could add to the list almost indefinitely. You may find two different games, like "Monopoly" and "Speeding," that are about the same topic but are presented with different ingredients mixed in. That way, you can choose the one that best suits your taste.

To keep you off the wrong path, there are also some "no-no" games. You need to know the kinds of games your neighbors are playing that are keeping them poor. You may even have been playing some of the no-no games yourself. Will you continue? It isn't likely, now that you'll know the truth about the games that can hurt you financially.

It really doesn't matter where you start. Pick a category that sounds interesting to you and just jump into that section of the book. Find some ideas that sound fun to you, start your saving process by trying the action steps, and have a blast doing it![3]

## *Where to Find the Answers to the "Vital" Money Questions*

How can I get rich while taking an afternoon nap? (See page 13.)

Can I really get rich with "pillow talk" and "quickies?" (See pages 14 and 21.)

Where is it dark at 10:30 AM and 9:00 PM? (See page 19.)

Who's Bob? (See page 20.)

Where can I get some free stuff? (See page 35.)

Should I change my name to Charlie? (See page 45.)

Is it better to be a duck or a goose? (See page 47.)

Do people really eat sawdust with lumps? (See page 64.)

Are bigger chests really better? (See page 202.)

Why do I need to own some **really dark** sunglasses? (See page 93.)

---

[3] Let me know how it goes. If you come up with some new games on your own, send me your ideas at newgameideas@wordsofabundance.com. I'll share readers' ideas on the Web site, and when I have accumulated enough new ones, I'll incorporate the best of them into *Money Games, Volume Two*. If you agree to have your game published, I'll see that you are credited for it and receive a free, autographed copy of the book!

How can I have happy money? (See page 151.)

How do you spell "vrooom?" (See page 158.)

Who's Uncle Wiggly? (See page 166.)

What's the one game neurotics always win? (See page 167.)

Is it time to find a new neighbor? (See pages 207–208.)

---

IF YOU DON'T HAVE MUCH MONEY NOW, BUT YOU
WOULD LIKE TO HAVE A LOT MORE IN THE FUTURE—AND
STILL HAVE PLENTY OF FUN IN THE MEANTIME—THIS
BOOK IS FOR YOU!

# ADVENTURE GAMES

# Restaurant Roulette

## Eat well; get rich?

Do you spend a lot of money eating out? In our fast-paced society, many of us do. If a sizeable portion of your budget goes toward dining out, as ours did, here's a game that will allow you to continue your habit—eating at great restaurants—but at a fraction of the cost. Interested?

Here's the first question: are there coupon books in your area that offer savings on fast food, fine dining, entertainment, and more? In our area, there are at least three competing discount books: *I-Dine, Discovery Dining,* and *Entertainment.* Each has coupons ranging from 10 or 20 percent off to "buy one, get one free" deals at local restaurants, movie theaters, and other entertainment venues. Some coupon books have hotel discounts as well.

So, what's the game? Buy one of the books, which typically costs twenty or thirty dollars. Then, next time you are ready to head out to a local restaurant, save some money by using one of the coupons. Here's a fun twist: open the book to a random page and try the restaurant you find on that page! This is a great way to discover new restaurants in your area while saving money at the same time.

Note: This is a game only for those who are already spending too much on dining out. If you are not in that category, this is not your excuse to join it now.

ACTION STEPS

1.  Look for discount books in your area.
2.  Peruse each one and find out which has the most coupons for the restaurants you frequent.
3.  Find someone to buy you that book for Christmas or your birthday.
4.  On an evening when you would normally pay full price at a local restaurant, pick a random restaurant for which you have a discount coupon.
5.  Use the coupon to save up to half of what you would normally have spent.
6.  Take the money you saved and set it aside in an account where it will accumulate interest until you have a large enough sum to invest it elsewhere.

# "Strip" Poker

## A fun way to get your friends to pay for your meals.

"Strip" as in magnetic strip, that is.[4] This game could also be in the "Card Games" section, since it involves credit cards. However, I've placed it under "Adventure Games," since it's a gamble whether or not you will win and save money or lose and pay more than your share. If you tend to be a lucky person, this game might save you some cash.

How to play: After you have finished a nice restaurant meal with friends (the more friends, the better), call the server over. Tell everyone at the table to hand over his or her credit card. Then encourage the server to put all the cards behind his or her back, shuffle them up, and choose one card at random. The owner of whichever card is drawn must pay the bill for the entire party.

For most people, this will even out over a long period of time, but it still adds some fun and excitement to an otherwise normal meal out with friends. For some of us, it has an uncanny way of saving us some money. Then again, we have one friend who has an unbelievable knack for having his card drawn more often than normal. He's frequently invited to our outings.[5]

If you "win" and someone else pays, go right home and set aside your savings (the amount you would have spent if you had paid for your own food) for your investment fund. Isn't it nice when your friends help you get rich?

ACTION STEPS

1. Have a nice meal at a local restaurant with friends.

2. Enlist the help of your waiter or waitress to take everyone's credit cards, mix them up, and blindly pull one card to pay for the entire group.

3. Pray your card isn't the one pulled.

4. Take the money you saved and set it aside in an account where it will grow with interest until you have a large enough sum to invest elsewhere.

---

[4] Some of you were thinking something else, weren't you? There are *other* books with *those* games!

[5] If you tend to be "that guy," eat at home.

# BEDTIME GAMES

# Making Money while You Sleep

## Let your money work 24/7 so you don't have to.

The nice part about this game is that it involves almost no work on your part. Just set up any interest-bearing account (passbook savings, money market, credit union, etc.), put some money in, and let compound interest go to work for you.

How does compound interest work? Let's say you put money in your account and leave it there for a year. Because you have "loaned" the financial institution your money, they reward you by paying you some of their money as interest. The next year, you get to earn interest on your money again, but—here's the exciting part—you also get to earn interest on the money they gave you the first year. Their money is now making *you* money. Isn't that awesome?

Once that starts happening, you can smile every night before you float off into dreamland; your money and their money are out there, working for you and earning more interest while you sleep.

Do you have a day off and need an afternoon nap? You can safely head for the bed. Your money is working, so you don't have to.

ACTION STEPS

1. Set aside some money where it will earn interest.
2. Take an afternoon nap.

# Pillow Talk

## How to talk to yourself just after you close your eyes for the night.

Many of us talk with our partners before going to sleep. That's not so odd. If you want to be odd, consider having some conversations with *yourself* before you go to sleep. You can take a few moments each night to say some positive things to yourself. Such positive thoughts are popularly called affirmations. The really great thing about this "pillow talk" is that you don't even need a pillow! You can speak—or affirm—positive statements about money in your life any time, anywhere.

The things you talk about are very likely to show up in your life. (Yes, you are to say these things before they are actually true. The act of repeatedly saying them actually helps them *come* true.) Do you typically say things like "I never have enough money" and "I hate paying these lousy bills"? If so, you'll never get the financial rewards you really want.

Instead, learn to say, "I always have plenty of money" and "I love to pay my bills! When I do, I decrease my liabilities and increase my net worth." The more you say these phrases, the more your brain will work to find ways of making them come true in your life.

Here are some great positive-abundance affirmations you can use:

1. "All my investments are successful and benefit everyone involved."

2. "I always have everything I need. Abundance flows to me simply and naturally."

3. "New ideas come to me effortlessly when I need them. God reveals them to me whenever I ask and remain open to following his lead."

4. "Through God's unfailing grace and his perfect timing, all sorts of abundance arrives in my life. I am quick to express my thanks for all good things."

5. "I always have plenty of money."[6]

---

[6] I have no idea who to thank for this marvelous phrase, but know I didn't originate it. I heard or read it somewhere along the line, and it has always stuck with me as one of the easiest, most useful phrases I've ever come across. To the originator, thank you, whoever you may be.

6. "My income increases as I share my abundance. The faster I give, the faster new and increased abundance shows up in my life."

7. "I enjoy bountiful abundance and give thanks for it continually."

8. "My wealth and abundance increase twenty-four hours a day, whether I am at work, at play, or at rest."

9. "As I open myself to God's guidance, I find myself exactly where he wants me to be and am profitably engaged in just the right activities."

10. "My value to the world and the abundance I enjoy increase in wonderful ways as I learn and grow every day."

11. "There is always more money in my life than I need because I give from my heart and freely allow God to direct my actions."

12. "I enjoy a financial life of ease and am free from worry."

Warning: Do not underestimate the power of this game. I have had friends make only this one change in their lives and completely transform their finances. Be careful to speak aloud *only* what you want to be true in your life. This technique works and has tremendous power. Stay completely aware of what you are saying about money.

## ACTION STEPS

1. Have a good talk with yourself each night before you go to sleep.

2. Talk aloud!

3. Say only things that you want to be true.

4. Let your brain and the universe take it from there.

# BORED GAMES

# Cheap-Show Movies

## It's the same movie! (And it's still dark in here.)

Are you an entertainment junkie like we are? My wife and I love going to the movies. But have you noticed how expensive they are getting? In our area they can cost more than ten dollars per ticket during prime time in the evenings. If you add in popcorn and water or soda and other snacks, the cost really adds up—especially when you see at least one movie each week, as we like to do.

So what's the game? Enjoy the same entertainment earlier in the day! We've found that they actually play the exact same movies at 10:30 AM as they do at 9:00 PM. Isn't that amazing? And it's actually just as dark in the theater at 10:30 AM as it is at 9:00 PM. You'll never know the difference. So save yourself a few bucks, go to the early show, figure out how many dollars you saved, and then go home and set aside that money for your investment account.

Bonus: Now that you'll have more evening time available, you can spend more time on pillow talk!

Another option: As the price of DVDs steadily decreases, we've found ourselves more frequently buying or renting DVDs and having popcorn at home. You can often purchase a DVD for less than the price of two movie tickets, and having popcorn at home is far less expensive than buying theater concessions. Best of all, you can see your favorite movies multiple times without incurring extra costs!

ACTION STEPS
1. Find out if the theater really is as dark at 2:00 PM as it is at 7:00 PM. If you're going to the theater, go to the early show.
2. Or wait for the DVD, and ...
3. Support Orville Redenbacher.

# Go Fish

## One pole, two boots, and say hello to Bob.

This version of "Go Fish" is the literal one. Grab a fishing pole, head off to a local stream or lake, and spend some time casting about. Activities like fishing fall into the category I call "reusable entertainment." You have some initial expenses when you buy your fishing pole and fishing license, of course, but after that, your entertainment is virtually free!

Find a hobby of your own that you greatly enjoy but that only has minimal ongoing costs. Hiking is another good example. Buy the hiking boots once, and you can have months and months of free entertainment, not to mention some great exercise. Better yet, buy the hiking boots *and* the fishing pole and hike to that remote fishing spot that most anglers won't try for. Those trout are just waiting for you!

If you go, say hello to "Bob" for me. (I called him that because I was using a "bobber," and he just wasn't buying the whole thing. He's probably still there in the North Fork of the Big Thompson River in Colorado. Let me know if you want more specifics.)

Now, don't go hog wild on me. You don't need eight poles, sixteen kinds of lures, forty-seven kinds of flies, four pairs of waders, fishing licenses for all fifty states, thirteen pairs of hiking boots, and seven "lucky shirts." One pole, a hiking boot for each foot, and some worms you dig up on the bank of the stream will work just fine. (I can let you know where I planted the worms, if that would help.) In this game, there are no hogs, just fish. We'll save the pigs for some other game.

ACTION STEPS
1. Buy a fishing pole, borrow one, or find one in the garage, attic, or basement.
2. Get a fishing license if you need one.
3. Find something wiggly (like a worm).
4. Go fish.

# Makin' Whoopee

## A retirement "quickie."

Wouldn't it be nice to have a safe, secure retirement filled with abundant income—enough that you can spend your time concentrating on "makin' whoopee" and/or having "quickies?" (If those don't ring a bell for you, ask someone old.)

Having plenty of money for your retirement is a "Whoopee!" event in and of itself. Here's my quickie lowdown on how and why some folks' retirements are WRECKs and why other folks seem to enjoy NICE TRIPs. Those who wreck are simply "Wrongly Responding to Everyday Common Knowledge." Those who have nice trips have "Necessary Information Coming Efficiently to Result in Prosperity!" Here are my quickie explanations for why folks end up with one result or the other:

**Four Reasons People Retire without Ample Cash** (The Wrecks)

1. They never think about prosperity or make conscious decisions to achieve wealth.
2. They procrastinate.
3. They never spend time learning how to obtain, invest, and protect money.
4. They are unable to delay gratification.

**Six To-Do Items to Guarantee a Cash-Filled Retirement** (For Nice Trips)

1. Decide to be wealthy; set specific long-range and short-range financial goals, and make detailed monthly, weekly, and even daily plans.
2. Save between 10 and 20 percent (or more) of your income throughout your life.
3. Invest wisely. Spend as much time learning how to invest and protect your money as you do learning to earn it.
4. Get rid of all consumer debt and stay rid of it.
5. Once you begin accumulating money, leave it alone!

6. Stick with your plan. Know that wealth building is a long-term game plan. Expect to spend ten, twenty, or even thirty years achieving your financial goals.

ACTION STEP

1. Reread and practice the six "to-do" items above. Action steps don't get any more concise than that.

# "CARD" GAMES

# AAA

## One card, free stuff, and lots of discounts.

Auto Club gives you a nice little plastic card when you sign up for its emergency road-service benefits, at least in California. Free gas plus free towing plus free jump starts equals one nice deal. In addition, you can get lots of extra "free" stuff[7] like maps, travel planners, and advice about hotels and restaurants just by asking.

But did you realize that this same card will often get you discounts at hotels, major amusement parks, and more? It will also get you discounts on rental cars. If you are a frequent traveler, don't forget to ask if the items you are purchasing or renting are eligible for a AAA discount.

Me: If you do get a discount, what do you do with the money you save?

You: Set it aside for saving or investing?

Me: Very good! You are catching on. Every time you find a way to reduce your expenses as a result of these games, take the money you save and set it aside so it can grow. You will be amazed by how much adds up over time.

If you're going to pay the fee for the card, why not make a game of finding enough ways to use it that you more than offset its cost? As with many of the other games, of course, be careful you don't start spending more money just to save more money. We're out to reduce expenses, not add to them.

Finally, if you are really enterprising, start thinking about how you can combine some of these games. If you've been reading from the beginning, you'll see how you can combine AAA with "Go Fish," for example. Check out how we can now combine action steps:

ACTION STEPS

1. Plan a trip to Colorado (near the North Fork of the Big Thompson River would be especially good).

2. Save on hotel costs and on your rental car with your AAA card.

3. Find your way around with the free maps from AAA.

4. Get a free jump start from AAA on your "Rent-a-Wreck" rental car, which really is a wreck. (But it is cheap!)

---

[7]    Free after you've paid your dues, of course.

5. Charge your other expenses, including the out-of-state fishing license, on your credit card, which you will pay off immediately upon returning home.

6. Have fun for days using the same pole and boots.

# Go Fish II

## Cross the "bridge" with lots of "hearts" and you'll be in "spades."

Yes, this time "Go Fish" refers to the card game that is so popular with young kids. However, the idea is much broader.

Consider how many games you can play after you purchase a simple deck of cards. There must be more than a hundred: bridge, spades, hearts, solitaire, cribbage, and so many more! And every time you play cards, you are making a wise financial decision—unless, of course, you are playing poker for money and losing.

How does playing cards help your finances? You are using a form of entertainment that has zero cost once you have purchased the deck of cards. Zero cost entertainment is always a winner. Set aside that money that you would have spent at the movies or elsewhere and invest it. You'll have fun twice over—fun playing cards and fun investing the money you save.

ACTION STEPS

1. Buy a deck of playing cards or ask someone for a set they don't use.

2. See how many different card games you can learn.

3. Cheat and win. (Just kidding on the cheating part …)

4. Take the money you would have spent on expensive entertainment and put it in an account where it will grow with interest until you have a large enough sum to invest elsewhere.

# Let's Make a Deal!

## The best invention since electricity–
## and it's worse than a tornado.

So what's your opinion on credit cards? Are they the best inventions since electricity or dangers worse than tornadoes? Most of us would choose the former, right? How else could you go out and buy a $1,000 item with only pennies in your pocket and then have the privilege of using it while you are paying for it?

The payments are *so easy*. Many cards only require monthly payments of 2 percent of your balance. Think of it—you can enjoy that $1,000 item for only $20 the first month and then less every month after that. Those lenders must be crazy to let you get away with that! Am I right?

Well, let's have a little mathematical test here. If you charge $1,000 at an annual interest rate of 17.3 percent and pay off 2 percent of your balance every month, how long will it take you to pay off the loan? Most people guess four or five years. But do you want the sobering truth? You will still owe $935 after one year, and you will need more than *twenty years* to pay off the loan entirely! It makes you think twice about buying that $1,000 item, doesn't it?

You know who's getting rich off that deal, right? (Hint: It isn't you!) The next time you are tempted to make that kind of purchase, call me! Instead of lending you the $1000 at 17.3 percent, I'll only charge you 16.3 percent! That's still not good enough? Okay, let's make a deal. You can probably talk me down to 15 percent if you really work at it.

ACTION STEPS

1. If you use credit cards, pay them off in full every month.
2. If you can't pay them off all at once, consider these options:
   - Pay as much as you can every month. Do you really want to be paying for that new couch twenty years from now when you've already given it to the Goodwill eight years before that?
   - Call your credit card company and ask for a lower rate. This works especially well when you've gotten a better offer in the mail from another

credit card company. Ask your credit card company to match the offer you've received.

- If your credit card company won't lower its rate and you have an offer for a better one, switch companies!

- If all else fails, call me. I have money available at 15 percent. (Besides, if you are that desperate, we need to talk anyway!)

# The Discover Game

## How to make money with plastic.

This is a game you play with one of your *plastic* cards. Be cautioned that it is good only for those with great discipline, but if that's you, this game can be very "rewarding."

As you probably know, Discover, American Express, State Farm Bank, and many other credit card companies pay you cash back from all your purchases. If—and only if—you pay your credit card bill in full every month, thus incurring no interest charges, using a rewards card can be a nice way to enhance your financial well-being. Here are the rules:

Rule 1: Pay for everything you can possibly think of using your rewards card—groceries, restaurant bills, gasoline, entertainment, you name it.

Rule 2: Pay every credit card bill in full when you receive it.

Rule 3: Use the cash back to either increase your investments or decrease your debts.

You can even make large purchases this way, assuming you have the cash set aside in advance. We have friends who purchased a new car and put the $5000 down payment on a rewards card. They already had the down payment set aside in their savings account, so putting it on their credit card just allowed them to increase the cash they got back.

You will "Discover" that a substantial amount of cash will come back to you. Do you feel like that $4 cappuccino is too small to put on the Discover card? Think again. If you make that same $4 purchase every weekday for a year, leaving out vacation weeks, you will spend $1,000 on cappuccinos. (Gosh, that's scary—maybe you don't need that daily cappuccino after all. Think what that $1,000 could do for you over time …)

After every purchase you make with your card, immediately "deduct" that amount from your checking account so the money is set aside to pay the credit card bill when it arrives. (This is a great idea anyway, even if you aren't playing the "Discover Game!")

Warning: Unless you are 100 percent certain that you can maintain perfect discipline while playing this game, don't play it. Even one month's interest charges on a balance not paid in full will negate all your fine efforts for the rest of the year.

Also, just because you are playing the "Discover Game" doesn't mean you need to go out and buy every widget, gadget, and doohickey just to increase your cash back at the end of the year. Forgo buying the gadget and put the money you would have spent into savings/investing instead. You'll thank me someday.

A last word of advice: Shop around for the best credit card. Discover doesn't pay 1 percent from the first dollar spent. Some cards do and may pay even higher percentages on purchases from gas stations, grocery stores, drug stores, or other specific retailers. Learn to read the fine print. Pay special attention to what happens if you make a late payment or accidentally miss a payment. You could lose your cash back, pay a large penalty, and have your interest rate increased. Yikes! This is one place it definitely pays to be well informed.

## ACTION STEPS

1. Avoid this game unless you are 100 percent disciplined and will pay your credit card in full every month.

2. Shop around for an excellent rewards credit card.

3. Put as many (necessary) purchases as possible on the card.

4. When you get your cash back, go blow it on frivolities. Ha! Had you going there, didn't I? Actually, you know the refrain by now ...

5. Take the money you get back and put it in an account where it will grow with interest until you have a large enough sum to invest elsewhere.

# COMPUTER AND
# SPY GAMES

# Browsing Around

## Gain some sense, save some cents.

Do you like the word "free?" Does it make your heart beat just a little faster, dilate your eyes, and make adrenaline surge through your body? Well, here's some good news. You can get lots of stuff free if you are willing to spend some time browsing around on the Internet![8]

Here are some sites to get you started, along with the descriptions of each that appear on Google.com[9]:

www.refdesk.com/free.html
Links to freeware sites and pretty much everything else that is free.

www.freebiefanatic.com
Choose from a huge selection of free stuff for your home and family.

www.producttestpanel.com
Test products. Voice your opinion. Receive new products and incentives.

www.thefreesite.com/
Offers free stuff including free samples, fonts, games, graphics, mobile phone items, anonymous browsing services, Webmaster freebies, and e-mail services.

www.totallyfreestuff.com/
TotallyFreeStuff.com is the largest directory of freebies online. Our freebie list includes free posters, software, T-shirts, mouse pads, clothing, hats, etc.

www.freecycle.org/
A grassroots and entirely nonprofit movement of people who are giving (and getting) stuff for free in their own towns.

www.volition.com/
Give in to your "volition" to get free stuff. This site will lead you to hundreds more sites with free products. This place is trial-sample heaven.

---

[8]  Just bear in mind that you may have to give up some of your privacy to get them.

[9]  Your author is not endorsing any of these sites. Some require you to be at least eighteen years old. Enter the sites and give out your information at your own risk. You're a big kid now. You are the responsible party.

www.1freestuff.com/
Offers free stuff such as free samples, health and beauty products, magazines, home-page building, freeware, food and recipes, and products for babies and kids.

www.freakyfreddies.com/
Free stuff for everyone; more than seventy-one categories of freebies updated daily.

www.Eversave.com
Sign up and get free stuff, including samples and coupons from top brand names.

www.ivillage.com/promotions/
Free stuff; shop, compare, and save. Find more than two hundred coupons and special deals from your favorite stores all in one place.

www.nojunkfree.com/
No Junk Free has always believed in bringing you the best freebies available on the web.

www.bestfreestuffonline.com/
Links to free makeup samples and free stuff for moms, dads, kids, babies, and pets.

www.freesitex.com/
Secret free stuff and free services on the Web that companies don't want you to know about. Secrets include how to get free Internet access!

www.freestufftimes.com/
Links to free stuff with archive and forum.

www.free-stuff.com/
Free-Stuff.com is an amazing collection of free stuff, freebies, coupons, downloads, magazines, and family stuff.

www.ofree.net/
Only oFree offers the largest collection of various free stuff and freebies, including samples, bags, magazines, computers, CDs, DVDs, books, gift cards, etc.

www.onlyrealfreestuff.com/
Order real free stuff and real free samples. No shipping, no handling, no cost to you, period.

www.freevault.com/
Get totally free stuff, free samples, free insurance quotes, free credit reports. FREEVault.com: Where you find all things free.

ACTION STEPS

1. Agree that the author has no legal responsibility for your using these sites.

2. Try some of the above sites to see if they are still there—they change frequently!

3. Do an Internet search for "free stuff." When I searched, I got ninety-one pages of hits. The sites listed above are just a tiny sample.

4. Remember that your privacy is at stake. Then again, your wallet may stay fatter as a result of your new free stuff, so maybe you're okay with that.

5. If you save some money by getting free stuff that you would normally have needed to purchase, you know what to do. Right?

6. Do not pass go. Go directly to jail if you stole your "free stuff" from your neighbor's house. If you came by your free stuff legitimately, go immediately to step seven.

7. Take the money you saved and put it in an account where it will grow with interest until you have a large enough sum to invest elsewhere.

# CEO/I Spy

## Pretend you are with the FBI or CIA.

What if Bill Gates, while he was CEO of Microsoft, had held a press conference and said, "Microsoft is losing money, and I don't have a clue why. I just don't know where it all goes." How confident would you have felt about the long-term prospects for Microsoft? Would you have been willing to invest in their stock? No! Would you have thought, "Wow, maybe it's time Microsoft got a new CEO!" Of course you would have.

Now take a minute and think about the CEO of *your* money. Who's in charge of keeping track of your money? Unless you are exceptionally rich and can hire someone else to do it, it's very likely that you're doing it yourself. Well, do you ever get to the end of a week or a month and say to yourself, "I just don't know where it all goes!" Hmm. Maybe you need a new CEO too! Or maybe you just need a better system for keeping track of the bucks coming in and the bucks going out.

One of the fundamental principles of wealth building is keeping a close watch over your finances so that you always know where the money is going and how much you are spending. All of us have our major expenses. Your list might include Starbucks, Krispy Kremes, candy bars, sodas, pizza, beer, DVDs, and shoes, for example. As CEO, could you tell me exactly how much you are spending in each of those categories? Most of us have rough ideas of how much money we spend on the major expenses like rent, mortgages, and property taxes, but somehow, there are always chunks[10] of money that just seem to disappear without a trace. What can be done?

If you are computer-savvy and enjoy spending time in front of the laptop or desktop, why not try out one of the money management software programs such as Quicken or Microsoft Money? These programs are excellent tools to help you categorize and keep track of your spending.

Wouldn't it be better to know from month to month exactly where your money is going? I bet Uncle Bill (Gates) knows *exactly* where his money goes. If it's a good enough plan for a billionaire, it might work for us too!

---

[10] "Chunk"—that's one of my favorite financial terms. It means "a lot more than a little, but less than a zillion."

Okay, I can hear you saying, "Well, that's all fine and dandy, but I can't carry my computer around with me wherever I go." Point taken. So find a tiny little pad and a tiny little pen or pencil that you *can* carry with you and record every single penny you spend all day every day. Transfer it to your computer later.

I also hear some voices saying, "I don't have a computer," and "Machines and I just don't get along." That's okay. You can buy inexpensive ledgers at office supply stores that will work just as well. The game isn't built around technology; it's built around tracking.

"But I just can't see myself doing this forever!" Don't worry—it's only for a short time. Within a month or two, it will be obvious to you (perhaps painfully so) just where the leaks are. Then you can decide whether you want to continue spending your money in those categories or not. You'll still be making the decisions. However, you will make *informed* decisions, and informed decisions are always better.

A nice bonus if you use software: Quicken and Microsoft Money are also excellent programs for tracking your transaction-intensive activities like buying mutual funds and reinvesting the dividends. When it comes time to sell, they can easily give you all the information you need. What used to be a complete pain in the arse (French for "mule") is now easy as can be.

What's that? Using Quicken doesn't sound much like a game to you? Okay, so think back to that tiny little pad and pencil. You can even pretend you are with the FBI or the CIA. When you are actually just writing down your financial transactions, look furtively around the Starbucks you are in. Pick a particular customer and glance back and forth between the customer and your pad as you write. They may never come back to that Starbucks again!

Two warnings: First, if you're going to go to Starbucks and do this every day, you may want to sell the Starbucks stock you own before you start this game. There may be *lots* of customers who stop coming. Second, be careful whom you pick for those glances. Personally I wouldn't pick that guy who's about six foot five, 260 pounds, and built better than most gorillas. If you think you're "broke" now …

## ACTION STEPS

1. Call Microsoft and see if they are happy with their current CEO.
2. Keep track of your expenses so you'll know exactly "who flung the chunk."
3. Find a tiny little pad and a tiny little pencil to set up your "Uncle Bill" plan.
4. Check your "arse" to see if the "Pain-B-Gone."
5. Watch out for gorillas.

# The GEEK Game

## It's a game where the family geek becomes the family hero!

Are you or your significant other a GEEK? That is, someone who "Gets Everyone Excited about Kash?" (You thought I was going to use it in a derogatory way, didn't you? Nope! As you'll see, the geek will soon become the hero of this game.) All kidding aside, if there *are* people in the adult portion of your family who really like dealing with numbers and enjoy computers, have them try this game; they'll like it! (You will too, as the game results in your wealth increasing.)

We've talked already about computer programs like Quicken and Microsoft Money. The first step in this game is to use one of those computer programs and teach your geek how to "hide" money. Yes, I am serious. Have your geek use your computer to hide some money! Whenever you make a purchase on one of your cash-back credit cards, immediately come home and have your geek deduct the sale amount from Quicken and put it in a special, hidden account where it will stay until the credit card bill arrives. That way, you will always have exactly enough set aside to pay each month's bill, and you will always know your running balance of cash that's available for other purposes.

If you are required to play "Tell the Geek" each night at dinner, which consists of relating your credit card expenditures for the day, you will find yourselves spending less with your credit cards. There is something about having to "fess up" that might make you think twice about spending to begin with.

It is worth repeating the benefits of this game. By subtracting the amount of your purchases from your bank account and hiding the money in another account, two things will happen. First, you will always know just how much money is still available for other monthly expenses—the geek can tell you each day. And second, when the credit card statement arrives, your geek will smile and tell you, "No sweat. We already have all the money set aside to pay the bill." (Let's see some smiles all around.) It really is exciting and stress-reducing to receive each credit card statement and know you have enough available cash to pay the bill.

The other important thing to realize is that "hidden" money is money that tends not to be spent. So why not take this game a little bit further and hide some money even though it *hasn't* been spent?

Say you went to the grocery store and saved money by using coupons and the Club Card from the store. Maybe you saved $4.76 by doing that. Tell your geek to subtract that $4.76 from your checking account and put into a secret "holding for investments" account. If you hadn't used the coupons and Club Card, that $4.76 would have been gone, right? So pretend it really is gone. Hide it away for investing. When the hidden investment account gets large enough, take the money out and go invest it! You'll be amazed by how fast the money will grow when you "Get Everyone Excited about Kash."

The nice thing about investments is that they are generally "out of sight" except when your monthly statements arrive. For us, "out of sight" also means "out of mind." It isn't as easy to get at the money in your investment accounts as it is to get cash out of the ATM, so you are much less likely to spend it.

ACTION STEPS

1. Find a geek.
2. Hide some money.
3. Get rich.

(See? I told you the geek would be the hero.)

# CRITTER GAMES

# Charlie Bird

**You might want to go take a shower before reading about this game; you are about to "come clean."**

There are two Charlies in this story: a lady I know named Charlie and Charles (Charlie) "Bird" Parker Jr., an American jazz saxophonist.

First, let's talk about the jazz Charlie. (He died when I was not yet two years old, but I've talked to him since, and he said it was okay if I called him Charlie for this game. Even so, I'll bow to his more common nickname and call him "Bird.") Bird was not only a saxophonist but also a composer—a creator. His contribution to jazz was so great that he is often compared to such legendary musicians as Louis Armstrong and Duke Ellington. In fact, some consider him to be the greatest saxophonist of all time.

Bird left a wonderful legacy with his contribution to jazz. What many people don't know is that that legacy almost didn't happen. You see, Bird had a heroin habit and drank heavily, a combination that nearly ruined his life and his career. Thankfully, he was eventually hospitalized for some months, came out clean, and proceeded to do some of the best playing and recording of his career. What's my point? Bird was messed up, but he figured it out, got help, and completely turned his life around.

I hope that you aren't a heroin addict, an alcoholic, or otherwise medically impaired, but if your *financial* life is messed up, let Bird be your example. Whatever your circumstances are today, you can improve them. Your biggest successes with money still lie ahead.

The other Charlie, a lady I know, is living proof of that. She never had problems with drugs or alcohol, and she thought she was doing okay financially. After all, she had a big inheritance coming some day to use for her retirement, she had a good job and could pay her way from month to month, and she knew that her wonderful Uncle Sam (the United States government) would help with Social Security some day.

The only thing Charlie didn't consider is that things in this lifetime have a way of shifting gears and changing up on us unexpectedly. What she learned (albeit the hard way) is that inheritances sometimes vanish (oops, there goes the retirement money) and that seemingly stable jobs can suddenly become uncertain or disappear (whoa, there goes the monthly income!). Good old Uncle Sam wasn't so

45

reliable either. First he raised the age at which she could receive benefits. Then he started talking about the possibility of reducing her benefits and/or taxing them more heavily.

Now, it's not as if Charlie needed to be hospitalized, but she did require some "treatment" of the mental variety. This wake-up call taught her that she needed to be planning to take care of herself and her family, not relying on others to fill in the gaps. Charlie just needed some education!

Whatever your present circumstances are, know that they can change. Plan as if they will change for the worse, and you will always be ready, no matter what happens. Act as though you won't get free handouts. Then think of how great it will be if you can handle life on your own and someone gives you a free handout anyway! Your tasty cake now has frosting.

You can initiate positive changes in your life. Make some beautiful music! Compose your life in a way that is not only self-sufficient but also leaves a legacy behind for others to appreciate and enjoy for years to come.

The world *needs* a few more Charlies.

## ACTION STEPS

1. Stay away from heroin and other addictive substances.

2. Soar along in good health and try to avoid the hospital.

3. Cover your tail feathers with insurance to handle the really big catastrophes that you can't handle on your own.

4. Stop hanging around the aviary looking for free handouts. Learn that any help you expect from others (including your Uncle Sam) may unexpectedly disappear.

5. Make your own way.

6. Plan as though you won't receive any inheritance.

7. Plan as though Uncle Sam won't pay your Social Security.

8. Plan as though you will have to be self-sufficient.

9. Change your name to Charlie.

# Duck, Duck, Goose

## If you get one of these in the mail, you'd better duck, or you'll be the goose.

If you like to fly low (take big risks), make a big splash (impress others with the large amounts of money you spend), and generally just "wing it" through life, this game is not for you. If those descriptors fit you, your finances are probably already fodder for someone's joke book.[11]

For this game you will need a pad of paper, something to write with, this month's pile of unsolicited mail, and a magnifying glass. (You might also want to procure a book on origami to learn how to make paper ducks in case you get bored.)

In this game, you're going to collect every unsolicited credit card offer you get for a month. Then, with the magnifying glass, you will reveal the hidden mumbo jumbo in the fine print that you (and millions of your friends) never bothered to read.

Won't that be boring? Well, yeah, but only until you get your friends involved and see who can find the most outrageous offer—that is, the offer most stacked to make the lender fat and happy and make you one quacked-up honker.

Ready? Let's fly. Here are some of the offers I've received lately:

- 0 percent APR for on transferred balances;
- 5 percent cash-back bonus;
- 4.90 percent fixed APR for 2 years.

Wow—those all sound amazingly good, don't they? However, thanks to your trusty magnifying glass, you'll notice that each of those three statements is followed by a small asterisk. Hmm. I wonder what nasty surprises those may be hinting at ...

Here's what I found out *inside* the envelopes:

First, they may tell you the card is 0 percent APR, but did you notice that they are going to charge you a 3 percent "transaction fee" on the balance transferred? Hmm, that's tricky. I'm not liking it.

---

[11] Question: Did you hear about the duck that landed upside down?
Answer: He quacked up.

Second, the 0 percent APR for life actually only lasts until you make just *one* late payment, even if it's only late by one day. Then (drumroll, please) the credit card company can immediately start charging you interest. Moreover, the interest rate (drumroll number two, please) can be as high as 28.99 percent. In addition—even better news—they can charge you a late fee as high as $39 on top of that! Am I kidding? I am not.

Third, the 5 percent cash-back bonus is never clearly defined, even in the fine print. Basically, it's 5 percent when *they* decide it will be for only as long as *they* think they should give it to you, and it only applies to select purchases from "partners" *they* decide on and change four times a year. Since when should you have to spend your money when someone else says to and only in the places they say are okay?

Fourth, remember that 4.9 percent fixed APR for 2 years? The fine print says you might even be able to extend that APR *beyond* 2 years! How? By being a good little consumer and making certain specific purchases or taking cash advances during each billing period! Sure, they'll extend that nice interest rate if you keep adding to what you owe them! What nice people they are! Not.

Were those credit card offers addressed to Mallard Fillmore, by chance? Well, you can see whose pockets are going to get the "Fillmore"—and they sure aren't *your* pockets!

Read the fine print. If it looks like a duck, walks like a duck, and quacks like a duck, then you'd better duck, because someone is trying to tempt you into accepting something that is not in your best interest.

Happily, not all credit card offers are poor ones. There are actually some nice online sites that rate and rank credit cards based on terms, rewards, etc. Every once in a while, you can find the goose that will lay golden eggs for you if you play exactly by their rules.

If you play "Duck, Duck, Goose," then once you find the goose, you can move on to the birds, horses, and pigs.

Oh, in case you're wondering—the pad of paper was for making the origami ducks, and the pen was to write the credit card companies your one-word reply ("NO!"). You can also use that magnifying glass to set those credit card offers on fire in the sunlight. Maybe this game was more fun than it seemed!

Special bonus: Web sites that rate credit cards

www.cardratings.com

www.e-wisdom.com

www.my3cents.com

www.creditcards.com

www.debtsmart.com

www.lowcards.com

## ACTION STEPS

1. Make sure your finances aren't in someone's joke book.

2. Read all the fine print.

3. Decide who's going to be fat and happy: you or the credit card company. (It's okay to be skinny and happy if you like that better.)

4. Have fun making origami ducks and burning stuff with your magnifying glass.

# Horse Poo

### It's a really "stable" game.

Are you feeling a little too "stable?" Do you happen to have a large property in the country? Why not board a horse? By the way, that's "board" in both senses.

You can board (keep) a horse by arranging to stable and care for someone else's horse on your property. Then you can really board (ride) the horse as part of your reusable entertainment.

Of course, fun and income aren't restricted to the equestrian realm. Many people have businesses for taking care of animals while their owners are away. These types of businesses sometimes offer care for pets right in the owners' homes. (Maybe you can cash in and be a house sitter at the same time!)

If you are an animal lover, the opportunities to earn extra cash are abundant. You can be a pet sitter, a mobile pet groomer, a pet walker, or even own a mobile pooper-scooper business. One service I saw advertised had a catchy slogan: "Our business is taking care of their business."

For a number of years, my wife and I lived in Colorado with two dogs and a large yard that had snow on the ground for several months at a time. Let me tell you, once that snow thawed, I would *gladly* have paid someone to "take care of the business!" What two dogs can do in three months is unbelievable. An enterprising person in our subdivision could have really "cleaned up," if you catch my drift.

Many pet owners love having their pets but hate the work that having a pet entails. You can be around lots of animals and make lots of money at the same time. Nearly every pet owner has "pet peeves" that they'd happily turn over to you in exchange for some cash.

ACTION STEPS

1. Engage in heavy petting. (The animals, the animals!)
2. Turn pet peeves into pocket cash.

# Hummingbird

## Friendly fun with furiously flapping, feathered fowl!

There is a great deal you can learn from our tiny, furiously flapping, feathered friends! Let's review what we already know about them. Here is some information I found in the free, online encyclopedia Wikipedia:

Hummingbirds "are known for their ability to hover in mid-air by rapidly flapping their wings fifteen to eighty times per second (depending on the species). Capable of sustained hovering, the hummingbird has the ability to fly deliberately backwards or vertically and to maintain position while drinking from flower blossoms. They are named for the characteristic hum made by their wings.... Hummingbirds bear the most glittering plumage and some of the most elegant adornments in the bird world.... They also typically consume more than their own body weight in food each day; to do that, they have to visit hundreds of flowers daily. At any given moment, they are only hours away from starving. However, they are capable of slowing down their metabolisms at night or at any other time when food is not readily available.... Most hummingbirds ... migrate to warmer climates in the winter."[12]

Okay, so we'll agree that hummingbirds are very impressive. What does all that have to do with improving your financial life? Let's think it through.

*Hummingbirds are known for their ability to hover in mid-air.* Lesson: Sometimes the best action is no action. If you are uncertain about which direction to take, especially if you are considering an expensive, large purchase or are contemplating how to best use specific dollars of your income, take your time. Hover. It's great to take action and to move fast, but be sure you've taken adequate time to consider your movements before you start.[13]

*The hummingbird has the ability to fly deliberately backwards.* Lesson: There will be times when you will make mistakes. If you've purchased stock and it has been slowly sliding down the slippery slope of loss, perhaps it is time to accept the loss

---

[12]  http://en.wikipedia.org/wiki/Hummingbird

[13]  Have you ever noticed that you never see hummingbirds zooming around at night? If you are going to head somewhere fast, you'd better be able to see where you are going.

and "deliberately fly backwards" by selling it. If you've made a mistake, admit it and correct it.

*The hummingbird has the ability to fly vertically.* Lesson: Sometimes you need to get up high to look at the big picture. We often get so mired down in our daily, weekly, and monthly routines that we forget to take time to review, think, and plan. Realize that you can get above your current circumstances. If you are lost in the woods, wouldn't it be useful to have a helicopter's view of where you are? If you could see your position from above, the path out of the woods would become clear. So go vertical. Keep your big goals in mind from up high, and you'll find that the daily decisions will become far easier.

*At any given moment, they are only hours away from starving.* Lesson: It's been said that most Americans are just two months away from starving. That is, that if all their income were to completely stop, in two months' time, many Americans would be broke.

Don't be one of *those* Americans! Set up an emergency fund. Financial fortunes change. Emergencies happen. Illnesses happen. Disabilities happen. Deaths happen. Water heaters go out. Washers and dryers break down. Basements flood. Hurricanes and earthquakes happen. Be certain that you have money set aside for the unexpected, and be sure to cover your largest potential losses (death, disability, long-term care, potential lawsuits, etc.) with adequate insurance.

*They are capable of slowing down their metabolisms at night or any other time when food is not readily available.* Lesson: Periodically review your expenses. Are there some that have gotten out of hand over time? Are you now subscribing to seven newspapers, twenty-one magazines, and six book clubs? Consider your cable and/or satellite television subscriptions. Have you added six movie packages, the high definition package, four deluxe sports packages, the adult channels (really?), or perhaps the "every channel in the universe" package? Where could you cut back to free up money for saving and investing? Slow down your "metabolism"—your consumption. If money is tight, overspending could be part of the problem.

*Most hummingbirds ... migrate to warmer climates in the winter.* One would assume that those who migrate early can stake out the best "territory." Lesson: Seasons change. High-performing investments change. Be sure you are diversified so that something in your portfolio is always doing well. Don't try to time the market. Just know that what's hot today may not be tomorrow. Look for the investments that no one wants today. Odds are that tomorrow someone will, and you can gladly sell yours to them when the time comes. Buy low, sell high. Buy an extra winter coat in July; sell it for double the price in December.

*Hummingbirds bear the most glittering plumage and some of the most elegant adornments in the bird world.* Lesson: If you are following the advice in this book and doing a great job of saving and investing, there will come a day when your wealth is beyond what you can even dream of today. Your investments will provide you with an income—without even touching the principal—that will allow *you* to have glittering plumage and elegant adornments, if that's what you wish.

*They are named for the characteristic hum made by their wings.* Lesson: Build your wealth secretly, stealthily, and steadily. You'll be smiling and humming your way through each day, leaving those around you to wonder what in the world is making you so happy. Won't that be fun? It's a bird! It's a plane! No—it's "humming man!" (Or "humming woman," if you are of the other gender!)

ACTION STEPS

1. Take time to "hover." When you're uncertain, pause for a minute. Move fast, but be sure you've given plenty of thought to your actions before you start moving.

2. Never be afraid to "fly backwards." If you've made a mistake, admit it and correct it.

3. Keep your big goals in mind constantly. It will make your daily decisions so much easier.

4. Set up an emergency fund and purchase adequate insurance for possible catastrophes. You are working hard to build your wealth; be sure to protect it as you go. Guard your territory.

5. Periodically review your expenses. Have they gotten out of hand? If so, make adjustments now! Don't wait for a crisis to prompt you into action. You'll make better decisions if you make them while you are not under pressure.

6. Diversify your portfolio. Times change. Investment performance changes. Have the "next best thing" before anyone else realizes that it is the next best thing. Bonus thought: Diversify yourself while you're at it! Companies make unexpected layoffs.[14] Have you developed broader talents that could give you an easy entry into a new career? If not, why not?

7. Plan ahead. Why shouldn't you have some glittering plumage and elegant adornments? Having a mental warehouse full of things you'd like someday is great motivation for saving and investing now.

8. Practice your humming. You are building an exciting, money-filled, well-protected future. Why shouldn't you hum with happiness?

---

[14] I should know. I spent twenty-eight years with a well-established national firm that had never laid off anyone in the history of the company. Guess what …

# Pig

**Don't go getting your hogback up. Just get the pig out.**

If you were offered a "pig in a poke," would you accept it? "Pig in a poke" is an old phrase some of you may not even recognize. It means something that's offered with its true value concealed. It represents a gamble, taking a chance, or possibly buying something sight unseen.

Are these good ways to spend your money? Not usually. Buying something sight unseen (some property "on the water" in Florida with "lots of friendly neighbors," for instance) can turn into a costly mistake. That property might turn out to be a tiny island surrounded by bayou … with lots of alligators for neighbors.

"But the salesman made it sound like such a good deal," I can hear you saying. Well, of course he did! You'd want to sell it too. But we both know that the only way that salesman was going to move that property was by concealing its true value—which is not much, unless you are a poacher and love to say, "See you later, alligator!"

There is really only one way to protect yourself from inadvertently buying a pig in a poke: taking the pig *out* of the poke so that you can see for yourself if it has value or not. How do you get the pig out? By doing something you've been doing ever since you were old enough for pigtails: increasing your education. Gosh, that sounds boring, doesn't it? I can hear you already: "Do we have to wallow through big, fat porkers of textbooks?"

Don't go getting your hogback up on me, now. If you keep being pigheaded, I'll send you back to the pigpen, and your pig-tale will turn into a real boar.

Instead, what if I give you permission to put some pig-ment (or color, especially *green*) into your bank account. Better yet, I offer you permission to protect the little piglets that are already *in* your bank account. How do you protect those piglets and add more pig-ment? Here's the secret: you have to have *knowledge*.

If someone offers you a poke (a sack or a bag, or in this case, some kind of an investment opportunity), you need to be able to look inside and know whether or not the bag is full of real gold or fool's gold. Knowledge is the only thing that will save you from mistaking one for the other.

The nice thing about knowledge is that there are many ways of attaining it. You can read those porkers of textbooks if you really want to (yeah right), or you can read some of the *fun* books about money, like this one! If you are an auditory learner, there are many books on tape, MP3s, and CDs related to money. Are you a visual learner? Try some of the many DVDs available. Attend seminars. Find a successful money guru and offer to buy him lunch if he'll share some of his hard-earned wisdom with you. (I'm available next Thursday.)

It doesn't matter how you take in information; just take it in. You need to learn about pigs, pokes, hogbacks, pigpens, and boars in order to create your own successful pig-tales and fill your piggy banks with paper covered in lots of green pig-ment. Oink.

ACTION STEPS

1. Protect the piglets.
2. Pork out on learning.
3. Buy me some lunch.

# Raptor

**It might as well be called "Cannibal,"
because someone wants you for dinner.**

Raptor is a "game," but it's not one you play in first person. Nonetheless, you need to know about it; if you are unwittingly involved in it, it will be as a game piece in someone else's game. Trust me, no good can come of that!

First, let's review what we know about raptors. Raptors are meat-eating birds that use their hooked beaks, strong feet, and toenails (talons) to catch and kill their prey. They eat mice, fish, snakes, and other small mammals such as rabbits. Another characteristic of raptors is their incredible eyesight, which is two or three times better than ours is. Some raptors can spot prey from more than a mile away, and others have such great night vision that they can hunt in the dark. Finally, many raptors have long, wide wings that let them soar on air currents and stay aloft for a long time without flapping their wings; their stillness helps keep their prey from noticing them.

Now, let's go back to the idea that you may be used as a "game piece." In Raptorville, this would make you a mouse, a snake, a rabbit, or a fish—someone else's lunch or dinner. Who could possibly think of you as lunch or dinner? Anyone who wants to steal away some of your hard-earned cash and use it for his own profit!

What's that? You want some examples? Okay, I'll give you some examples. Start by considering how many credit card offers arrive in your mailbox each year. I've never counted, but I think it could be as many as four or five per week, which adds up to more than two hundred in a year. Do all those credit card companies have your best interest at heart? Of course they do. Everyone knows that, right? After all, they are offering low interest rates (sometimes even 0 percent!), no payments for up to six or twelve months, and free checks that you can fill in and use immediately.

Let me ask again: do all those credit card companies have your best interests at heart? No! They are raptors. Each time you get a credit card offer in the mail, think of that hawk or eagle soaring silently above you, just waiting for you to make a move and accept the offer so they can swiftly swoop down and rip your cash right out of your pocket. They want to "catch" you and eat your money for lunch.

Remember, raptors have great eyesight. They can spot a sucker from a mile away, even in the dark. You know they've spotted you if you even receive their offers in the mail. And they've done it in the metaphorical dark if you even *consider* taking them up on their offer without reading the fine print. The fine print is where you discover whose interest they really have at heart. It's your interest, all right—the exorbitant interest you'll have to pay if you are ever even one day late with one single payment.

Of course, the credit card industry isn't the only industry with raptors at work. Stock brokerages also have the occasional raptor. Do you have money invested through a broker at a major firm? Does the broker seem to be moving your money from one investment to another with a frequency that makes you uneasy? You may have encountered a raptor. Who makes money each time your dollars are sold from one security and used to purchase another security? The broker does.

To be fair, not every broker is a raptor. As with every industry, there are wonderful, caring, knowledgeable representatives who have your best interests at heart. Just be sure yours does.

Are there raptors in my own industry, insurance and financial services? I'm sorry, but there are. There are raptors who sell you specific products because they are the products with the highest sales commissions, not the products that best suit your personal needs.

So how do you avoid being a piece in someone else's game? How do you avoid being suckered into a bad deal where the only person who *isn't* making any money is you? Here are some tips:

- Know that raptors like to catch the little guys. Who would an unscrupulous businessperson more likely go after: an uneducated person who has his guard down, or an educated person who is always vigilant?

- Raptors can easily spot prey in the dark. See that you are "enlightened" so their jobs will be more difficult.

- Raptors soar silently through the air, so never take a quiet sky for granted. Be wary.

## ACTION STEPS

1. Consider whether your "advisor" is spending 80 percent of her time with you asking questions and listening or 80 percent of her time talking and "advising" you. The advisor with your best interests at heart will spend the majority of her time learning about your dreams, goals, needs, and wants.

2.  Become educated. Learn how credit card companies make their money. Learn how your broker or financial services advisor is compensated. Learn about the wide variety of products available in the marketplace.

3.  Read the fine print. Take the time to examine every detail of every contract. Let that raptor have his lunch or dinner on someone else's dollars. Protect your own dollars as if they were gold, because they are!

# FAMILY GAMES

# Appreciation

## Enjoying FREE-dom.

Why not spend some time enjoying activities that cost little to nothing? How much does it cost to have a conversation with a wonderful friend? (Well, okay, so it might cost a bit for a couple beers or a little wine.) How much does it cost for a walk in the park or a stroll along the streets in your neighborhood? You can enjoy the sap dripping from the trees, be chased by bees, get dive-bombed by birds, or be chewed up by your neighbor's pit bull for an amazingly low cost: nothing!

We are surrounded by beauty, yet we spend so little time really slowing down enough to enjoy and appreciate it. There are lots of free parks, galleries, and exhibits. Have you even taken the time to explore the attractions within ten miles of your home? There are very likely parks you haven't been in, neighborhoods you haven't visited, stores you haven't window-shopped, historic monuments you haven't seen, and grouchy neighbors you haven't met. Odds are that someone vacationing in your area has probably seen more of what's around you than you have. Get out there!

Finally, make sure to spend time just appreciating the things you've accumulated. Are there DVDs you haven't watched in a long time? CDs you haven't listened to in months (or years)? Photographs you haven't perused in ages? When was the last time you stopped to appreciate the photos, artwork, and decorations in your own home? Try taking two weeks just to enjoy the things you have, making no outside purchases other than food. You already have many, many blessings. Why not take time to appreciate them?

ACTION STEPS

1. Get a map of your area.

2. Mark a ten-mile radius surrounding your home.

3. See how many fun (and free) things you can find to do in that area. (Watching the neighbors with binoculars doesn't count.)

4. Return home.

5. Count the ceramic Santa Clauses and snow globes you've collected (all 80,634 of them) and admire them one by one.

# The Garden Hose Game

**The whole family can play, but beware … it's a little kinky.**

Have you ever noticed what happens when a garden hose becomes kinked? The flow from the end of the hose is reduced or stops entirely. Even though there is plenty of water just waiting to flow out of the spigot, no water is able to get through because of the blockage.

The flow of money in your life functions in a surprisingly similar way. A variety of things can block or hinder the free flow of money through your life. Some of the blockages may seem to have no direct connection to money, but if you'll humor me and try unblocking them, I assure you that you'll be amazed by what happens to your wealth.

Here is the first surprise: Clutter blocks wealth. How could something as seemingly innocuous as clutter stop the flow of money in your life? No one really knows for sure, but my best hypothesis is that clutter is a distraction. You can't, for example, see a six-month accumulation of unread magazines and not feel some amount of distraction. For your money to really flow, you must be focused, and distractions interrupt focus. So get busy cleaning out those closets, cleaning out that garage, reading or getting rid of those old magazines, filing those ancient documents, and balancing those bank statements. The more clutter you remove, the more money flow you will notice. It may not seem logical, but I've seen it work time after time.

The second surprising piece of advice: Resolve any unresolved conflicts. Have you argued with someone recently and left on poor terms? Is there someone you've wronged who really deserves an apology? What about someone who's wronged *you* who you simply need to forgive? Unresolved conflicts block prosperity. Take steps to make them right, and watch good things start flowing into your life.

Here is the final surprise: Blockages also comes from things that are incomplete. How many projects have you started and then set aside partially finished? Many of us have projects like that, and they call out to be finished every time we see them, but we keep ignoring them. Have you started writing a letter but haven't completed it? Started reading a book and left it unfinished? Started a scrapbook or photo collection and left the project somewhere midstream? Incomplete projects are much like clutter and unresolved conflicts in the sense that they distract you from having a laserlike focus in your life.

Consider this analogy: One of your hereditary traits happens to be poor eyesight. To correct the situation, you get prescription eyeglasses. When the eyeglasses are properly cleaned, your vision is stellar. However, what happens when dirt and grime, smudges and smears start building up on the lenses? Your stellar eyesight vanishes.

Incomplete projects, unresolved conflicts, and clutter are all "gunk" blocking your perfect financial vision. Start completing them, resolving them, and cleaning them up, and you will be amazed by the way the flow through your financial garden hose increases.

There's not a strong logical connection, I know, but accept this challenge and see what happens. You are in for an amazing surprise!

## ACTION STEPS

1. De-clutter.
2. Resolve conflicts. (Start with a foreign country of your choice. We'd all appreciate it.)
3. Complete the uncompleted. (Finish this book, for example.)

# Twins

## It must be like eating sawdust with lumps.

Have you ever looked closely at identical twins? On close inspection, what do you generally notice? Yes, you've answered correctly—they aren't truly identical. There are differences, though they may be subtle. What seems identical at first glance really isn't.

Please head for your favorite grocery store. (Woo-hoo! This sounds like fun already!) When you get there, find one of your favorite brand-name products. Have you found it? Okay, look around. Is the same product being produced by competitors? Yes? Hmm. Thinking back to our twins, do you think the competing brands are all truly identical?

For years I would only eat the Raisin Bran that had two scoops of raisins. Those advertisers had me *convinced* that two scoops must be better. Not that I had any idea how many scoops were in the other major brand, but surely it must have been fewer than two, right? Then one day when I was really in a money-saving mood, I happened to notice a *third* brand of Raisin Bran on the shelves ... a *generic* brand. Unbelievably, it was almost *half* the price of my "two scoops" brand. "Wow," I thought, "for that price, it must be like eating sawdust with lumps!" Even so, I speculated that I surely wouldn't die from eating a week's worth of sawdust and dried lumps. Therefore, I bought the generic.

The next day, I prepared for the worst—I had extra sugar nearby. I took the plunge. Opening the generic box, I poured my first bowlful and began to eat. I casually ate four or five bites as I read the newspaper. Then, all of a sudden, I looked back at the box to be sure I'd really opened the generic. I couldn't believe it—I actually liked the generic *more* than I liked the "two scoops" brand I'd been eating for years! But for a long time, I'd actually hide the generic boxes when we had overnight company. I didn't want anyone to think I was so poor as to resort to generic Raisin Bran.

But since then, I've gone public; the Raisin Bran is out of the closet. This generic stuff is *great*, and it is nearly half the price. I'm saving 40 percent or more, and I'm happy to show you both how and why.

The whole Raisin Bran affair got me thinking. Was it possible that there were *other* name-brand items in my cabinets that might be just as good in generic form at a fraction of the price? With some searching, I discovered generic versions of vitamins, cold medicine, pain relievers, toiletries, bleach, coffee, salt, cleaning products, cheese, and dishwashing detergents. I even found the equivalent of generic wine. (We'll toast to that idea again in a later game.)

Are all the generics as good as or better than the originals? If you push me to answer honestly, no. I do have to admit, however, that a great many of the generics *are* just as good or better, and my spending has decreased amazingly since I've discovered them and started using them.

## ACTION STEPS

1. During the week, keep a list of groceries you need.

2. Head for the grocery store with your list in hand.

3. Optional: Ask a store employee where to find "sawdust with lumps." (This step is just to get you into the mood of the game.)

4. As you find each item, check the surrounding areas—especially the hard-to-reach areas—for generic versions of those same items.

5. When you find the generic items, ask yourself, "Am I brave enough to get rich?"

6. If your answer is "yes," take the generics home instead of your usual purchases.

7. Keep track of the money you are saving with each generic purchase. When you get home, set that amount of money aside in your savings account.

8. During the week, try the generics—they won't hurt you just this once. If you aren't pleased with them, you can always go back to your usual "get poor" brands next time.

9. Have a toast to your success with some generic wine (once I explain it in a later chapter).

# GEOGRAPHICAL GAMES

# Euphrates

## Toss me in. I'll find the pearl!

Do you believe that you can influence the quality and—better yet—the *quantity* of your finances just by changing your thoughts? Many people, some of whom are quite rich, believe this to be true.

Think about what happens in the physical world. If we plant carrot seeds, what happens? If we plant dandelion seeds (as if we have to), what happens? The ground returns whatever we plant in it. Why would our minds be any different? Whatever we "plant" in our minds, we'll get back in our circumstances. If we think thoughts of lack and low self-esteem, what will we get back? Does it cost any more to plant mental seeds of abundance and self-confidence? No. However, the results are vastly different.

Whatever your mind focuses on most will tend to happen. If you begin to expect wonderful events and experiences and abundance, that is exactly what will begin to flow into your life. Riches and prosperity will become your reality.

Let me reinforce that thought once more—whatever we plant in our minds, we'll get back in our circumstances. If you've been attracting debts and general financial disarray, start paying attention to your thoughts. It is very likely that your thoughts and your actions have both been wrong. As a result, what you have been attracting has also been off the mark. Why not change your thoughts so that they are positive and expectant? The ancient Babylonians had a great proverb: "If a man be lucky, there is no foretelling the possible extent of his good fortune. Pitch him into the Euphrates, and like as not, he will swim out with a pearl in his hand."

Do you believe you are lucky? Do you believe your financial well-being is always improving? Do you expect your net worth to constantly increase? What might change in your life if you thought that way? What could you possibly lose by trying?

ACTION STEPS

1. Think positive thoughts. (Think Euphrates. Think pearls.)
2. Take positive actions. (Dive in. Start looking.)
3. Watch every aspect of your financial life immediately begin to change for the better. (Find pearls.)

# Mississippi (MSI-MSI-YIPPEE)

## It's about Saint Bernards and garden hoses.

According to Wikipedia (the free online encyclopedia), "the Mississippi River has the third largest drainage basin (catchment) in the world" and "drains 41 percent of the forty-eight contiguous states of the United States. The basin covers more the 1,245,000 square miles" and "drains most of the area between the Rocky Mountains and the Appalachian Mountains."[15]

The fact that the Mississippi discharges so much water throughout the year (200,000 to 700,000 cubic feet per second!) is due to its numerous sources of inflow. Eighteen different sources contribute to the massive amount of water that the Mississippi moves over its 2,320 miles, including Lake Itasca, the Illinois River, the Missouri River, the Ohio River, and the Arkansas River.

Wouldn't you love for money to flow to you with the same incredible abundance that water flows to the Mississippi? It can! You just need multiple sources of inflow as well. For rivers, the inflow comes from tributaries. For you, it will come from what are called Multiple Streams of Income (MSI).

Imagine you have a large Saint Bernard (we'll name her Cindy) and an equally large metal tub in your backyard in which to bathe that Saint Bernard. How long do you think it would take to fill your metal tub using one small garden hose? That's an easy answer: quite a long time. However, what if you had four or five or ten garden hoses with which to accomplish that same task? You could have the tub filled in no time. This may not particularly thrill Cindy, but it would make the process much less time-consuming for you.

Next, we must also consider the diameter of each hose—are the hoses one-half inch or three-quarter inch? How much water can they carry? Are there any kinks in the hoses? To minimize the time required to fill the tub, we need the maximum number of hoses with the maximum possible diameters, and water must flow freely through each one.

Now take this analogy and compare it to your financial streams of income. How many different streams of income do you have? The most common answer is one: your job. The truly wealthy have learned to create more major income streams—the money that comes from the investing they do. Just like the Mississippi, the

---

[15]   http://en.wikipedia.org/wiki/Mississippi_river

flow of money from your investments will be strengthened by increasing the number of investments you have! The income you receive from investing can multiply and become a river in itself, fed by many individual streams: the mutual funds, bonds, stocks, and other assets in which you have invested.

At first, the income from your investments may be quite small, but that will change. If you are playing a number of the other games in this book at the same time, you will also be:

- paying off your debts;
- increasing your salary;
- making better and more appropriate spending choices;
- accumulating more money to invest.

As you get better at each of these activities, your second income (the one from your investments) will start growing with amazing speed.

In the meantime, why not start building some other tributaries for income? Are there some other ways you could build secondary income streams? You could develop an interest, hobby, or talent into a business that could produce income. (Writing this book is an example of that for me.) What unique abilities or hobbies do you have that you could use to produce profit? Some possibilities might be:

- photography;
- needlework;
- singing and/or songwriting;
- woodworking;
- painting;
- pottery;
- Internet auctions;
- writing (sounds good to me!);
- collecting (coins, hats, memorabilia ... there are hundreds of options);
- teaching about or repairing computers;
- cooking.

Almost any hobby or talent can be turned into a source of income with a little creativity. Some people also use real estate as a wealth-building tool. Reasons you might want to consider real estate investments include:

- the potential for returns that stay ahead of inflation;
- possible tax deductions (make sure to consult your tax advisor!);

- leverage (a small down payment can sometimes control a property with high value);
- population demographics (as long as the population is growing or moving, opportunities exist).

Remember the mighty Mississippi. It gains its enormous power from the tributaries that feed it. It has five major sources and up to thirteen lesser sources. How many sources of income can you develop? The more sources you have, the faster your wealth can grow.

## ACTION STEPS

1. Take a look at the income streams that are currently feeding your finances. Are they giving you enough inflow to save, invest, and live the lifestyle you want?

2. Consider your talents and hobbies. Could you turn one or more of those talents or hobbies into potential income streams?

3. Make a list of the steps you will need to take to begin turning your abilities into extra income. Then take the first step.

4. Remember the Mississippi. Build your own MSI (multiple streams of income), and more MSI, and you'll soon be saying, "Yippee!"

# MAGICAL GAMES

# Hocus-Focus

## Control your actions; change your results.

Do you know what you want to accomplish—for example, saving lots of money and achieving a million-dollar net worth—but find that time just seems to get away from you each day? This magical game will teach you *the one secret* guaranteed to help you overcome this problem. Follow this advice, and you may find that you make more progress in a month than you've made in the past year! What you are about to learn could revolutionize your life.

### The Secret to Improving Your Financial Life

Consider your present circumstances. How did you get into your current financial situation? You got there in exactly the same way the rest of us got into our present situations. Everything we have become, accomplished, or achieved is the result of some *action* we have taken.

In that statement is a marvelous truth. However, without some conscious thought, it remains so craftily hidden that it remains virtually a secret. Here it is: *Our results are always the consequences of our actions.* Every action has a certain result. This "secret" has tremendous potential power for you. Its power will be yours once you understand this idea: *By controlling your actions, you can change your results.* If you are not satisfied with your present financial situation, you can change it! If you want to be someone different or achieve something different, just *do* something differently.

To prove this concept to yourself, think about all your friends and see if you can identify two individuals who are equally intelligent and educated and have had roughly the same opportunities. (Maybe they even work for the same company.) Yet one of the two has advanced more rapidly than the other has, is making more money, and is happier and more successful.

Have you identified two people? Okay, now answer this question: Why, when everything else was relatively equal, did one person achieve so much more success? Have you guessed that it must have to do with the choices she made and the actions she took? Bravo! You are correct.

The odds are against finding our fortunes by winning the lottery. However, the odds turn dramatically in our favor if we just keep moving toward success in small steps every day. Reread those last two words. Say them aloud: "every day." Every day, you have choices—to do one more thing to move toward success or not. Become aware of your daily choices. Make the choices that will move you toward your most important goals.

"But I already know *what* to do," you insist. "There's just not enough time." Let's see if that's true. Remember the two friends you were thinking about earlier? Call them up and ask how many hours they have in a day. If the more successful one says she has twenty-eight or thirty hours, then that argument may be valid. (If that's true, I want her name and phone number!) If not, we're right back where we started. We must make better choices related to our time and our actions.

## Using the Prieto Principle to Improve Your Time-Management Skills

Have you ever heard of the Prieto Principle? It's the idea that 80 percent of something's value comes from 20 percent of the effort you put into it. Of all the things you do in the course of a day, 80 percent of your results come from just 20 percent of that day's efforts.

See if that's true. Make a list of all the activities you do in a normal business day. List *all* of them. If you socialize with friends, eat lunch in the cafeteria, or talk to your spouse on the phone during your day, those things should be on your list. Write down every activity you can think of. (I'll stop writing while you do that.)

Now review your list and identify the two or three activities that are the most critical to do if you want to obtain the financial results you want. Write those items down separately in no more than one or two words each.

Next, think through your typical day. How much time do you really spend doing those activities? If you are scrupulously honest, you'll likely say 20 percent or less. (If your percentage is substantially higher, I should be reading a book *you've* written!)

Can you see what a tremendous difference you could make in your personal effectiveness if you could increase the percentage of your time that you spend on your most important activities? I have no doubt that you do. So how do you do it?

## A Technique to Help You Focus

Each day, when you are prioritizing your tasks, write those one- or two-word descriptions of your most important activities above your list of tasks. Then prioritize solely based on which tasks match the items you wrote at the top of the page. In this way, you will be determining your daily priorities based on your two or three most crucial activities. Following this method greatly increases the probability that what you accomplish will be in line with what you value the most.

## Your Opportunities for Greatness

Every day you have opportunities to take small steps that will move you in the direction you want to go. Every choice you make will either move you closer to or farther away from success. Sailboats make a wonderful analogy for this concept. Two boats only yards apart and in the same wind can sail in opposite directions. Isn't that fascinating? How is that possible?

The answer is deceptively simple: it is all in the set of their sails. This principle also explains how two people with the same potential can exist under nearly identical conditions yet achieve vastly different levels of success. Choice—or how they have set their sails—makes all the difference.

We all have daily opportunities for financial improvement. If we fail to take advantage of them, it is only because we miss the choices that will move us in their direction. Become conscious of your choices. Focus your efforts on your most crucial activities. Then success will be yours every day!

ACTION STEPS

1. Know exactly how much money you wish to accumulate and the specific target date you have for achieving that goal.

2. Track how you use your time every day. How much of your time do you actually spend working to improve your finances?

3. Make small, daily choices that will move you closer to the financial goals you have set for yourself.

4. Become conscious of your choices and focus your efforts on your most crucial activities.

# Negotiation

## Are you ready for the seven magic words?

Try negotiating *everywhere!* You'll be surprised that many places will give you lower prices just because you ask.

I was in a well-known, discount electronics store, talking to a friend about a purchase I was about to make. I'd done my research and was informing my friend about the specifications of the item. Another shopper overheard our conversation, thought I was a store employee, and started asking me questions. I informed her that I wasn't an employee but helped answer her questions anyway. She wanted a similar item as a gift for her husband. The item I was looking at was slightly out of her price range, but she really liked it. I called over a salesman and told him that if we could get an additional discount on the item, he could sell two of them.

The salesman went to the store manager, and guess what? They actually *did* give us a discount on what was already a sale price. The lady got a nicer present for her husband, and I got a better deal. You just never know what will happen when you ask.

Would you like an easy, seven-word question that will work time after time to get you better deals? This question comes from Richard Paul Evans' book *The Five Lessons a Millionaire Taught Me* (Evans 2005). He calls these the Seven Golden Words—I call them the Seven *Magic* Words.

Here they are: "Is that the best you can do?" Just keep saying those same seven words until the person you are negotiating with finally says "yes." You'll be amazed by the amount you will save.

ACTION STEPS

1.  Practice your "Wow! I'm so happy! This is great!!" look in the mirror until you have it perfected.

2.  Hang out in electronics stores (or other purveyors of particular items you need).

3.  Hang out near nice ladies (or gents) who seem to know a lot about the product you want to buy and who may also want to make a purchase.

4.  Call over the store manager and ask if you can have a discount if more than one of you buys a particular product.

5. Use the seven magic words: "Is that the best you can do?" (Use them with the store manager, silly, not the other customers.)

6. When you get your reduced price, flash your well-practiced "Wow! I'm so happy! This is great!!" look at everyone in sight.

# Stardust

## The "Big Bang" and the Magic Kingdom.

A friend of mine was recently trying to explain the big bang theory to me. I didn't understand it before, and (sorry, Jean) I still don't. I understand that "big bang" means a giant explosion of some sort. Maybe it was like an extra-humongous megastar that exploded into a gazillion pieces that floated out and created the galaxies and planets as we know them over a bazillion years. (Am I close?) Somehow, apparently, we humans were formed by that event as well. Or maybe some amoeba was, and then it turned into a jellyfish, and the jellyfish morphed into a frog, then into an ape, then into a human.

I'm not a scientist (you noticed?), but one thing did seem interesting to me. If an explosion of a "star" started all that exists today, that would mean we're all made up of "stardust," in a sense. Now, I may not have a clue about the big bang, but if I'm made of stardust, well, that's pretty magical! (Though if you ask me what happened in the universe before I was born, I'll have to admit to having a slightly hazy memory.) And while I don't really have a clue what happened in the universe back then, it's a pretty good bet that if the big bang did happen, it was a *very* long time ago. Therefore, that stardust *must* be magical to have survived all these eons and arrived to form me today.

Can you remember at least a few moments in your life that you consider "magical?" For me, one involves the Magic Kingdom. I remember going to Disneyland as a child, going on the Peter Pan ride, and really believing I was flying. That event is still right up there on my personal list of magical moments.

Actually, childhood in general was pretty magical for me. It was a time to let my imagination run wild. What I could conceive, I could believe. I had a cowboy hat and a household broom, and using the broom as my horse, I galloped around the backyard saving the world as Roy Rogers riding Trigger. Today I'd probably be Harry Potter. Brooms are still cool.

What happened to all that imagination and magic and wonder that filled my (and hopefully your) childhood? Is it still there? My answer is yes! I think we've just forgotten how to believe in it, how to look for it, and how to practice it.

I digress, but I do have a point in mind. Let's go back to stardust. They say matter changes but that it never goes away. If that's true, that magical stardust from eons ago is still here, and we're all made of it! If so, we're not just magical beings, we're magical *eternal* beings. Our matter just changes over time.

So if I'm made up of millions of tiny bits of magical stardust, and if the matter we're made of will continue to exist throughout all of time, then we must be part of something eternal. If that's true, why am I here now? It seems there must be something magical that I'm meant to do while I'm in human form and an inhabitant of planet Earth. Guess what? I think *you* are meant to do magical things too.

You'll agree, I'm sure, that we are all capable of thought—which is pretty magical all on its own—and that we can use our thoughts to create many of the circumstances in our own lives. We can use our thoughts and "magical" energies in both broad ways (improving the planet) and specific ways (helping other humans).

All this reminds me of the book *Random Acts of Kindness* (Kingma and Markova 2002). It talks about the impact we can have by finding at least one thing we can each do anonymously every day for someone who will never be able to repay us. What great fun that is!

Okay, I digressed again. The point is this: whether we believe in the big bang or not, it is time for us to start realizing that our presence on Earth is truly magical. We can "wave our magic wands" and take actions that will improve our own lives and the lives of countless others on this seemingly lonely planet. (Though it can't be *that* lonely if everything else in the universe is made of stardust too!)

If we think of ourselves as eternal beings, at least in the spiritual sense, and we believe our thoughts and actions can affect others and ourselves, shouldn't we think twice about how we use our magical stardust every day? What have you done today to improve yourself? What have you done to improve the day for someone else? What have you done to improve the planet today? You are magical. Your impact is eternal.

If you can use your magic to create more income and more wealth, why would you want to waste that power buying more porcelain Santa figurines or your twenty-eighth Thomas Kincaid print, especially when the twenty-seven you already have won't all fit in your house now? Spend at least some of your magic in positive ways that might affect eternity. You may look back eons from now and be glad you did.

ACTION STEPS

1. Realize that your presence on Earth is truly magical.

2. Consider this: If you are truly an eternal, spiritual being, how are you "spending" the magic you've been given while you occupy your human body and brain?

3. Ask this: Will you leave this planet better than you found it? Will mankind be enriched by your passing through or just by your passing?

4. How many of the Earth's resources are you using? Are you using them wisely? There is a correlation between your wealth and the wealth of the planet. Help the planet, help yourself.

5. Spend at least some of your magic in positive ways that might affect eternity. We'll all thank you for it.

# The Magic Box

## Having one can completely transform your financial life.

Preface: Pay special attention to this game. In the money seminars I lead—in which I often present many of the same ideas you are reading—this is the one idea I consistently hear about from audience members weeks and months later. One participant went out of her way to call me just to say, "This one idea has completely transformed my financial life, and I just wanted to say thanks." Of all the games, this may well be both the most fun and the most powerful. I urge you to try it!

Getting prepared: For this game, you'll need some kind of a container that will hold money. An ornate, antique, wooden box adds to the fun and mystery of this game, but any container will do, especially one that can be closed or covered. A box, a jar, a large piggy bank, you name it. Take a minute and go find one. You can always shop the antique stores for a fancy one later if you like this idea well enough. I'll stop writing while you find your container. Let me know when you get back, and I'll continue.

All right, so you have your box. This box *becomes* magical as you use it, but if you want to enhance the experience by decorating it in mysterious, wizardly ways or adding a magic wand to go with it, by all means do so. Part of the magic comes from the fun the box generates as you use it.

Are you ready for me to quit messing around and just tell you what this darn box is for? Well, here you go—*the box is for the temporary storage of money waiting to be invested elsewhere.*

Disappointed? Don't be. When you really get this game rolling, you will not only have a blast, but you'll also save more money than you ever thought possible!

Getting started: Money gets into the box in two ways. Every single day—preferably first thing in the morning—you must add *some amount* of money to the box. It doesn't matter if the amount is twenty dollars, a nickel, a penny, a dollar, or twenty-three cents. You pick the amount, and whatever amount is handy will do. The important thing is not how much money is involved but that you do it *every day*.

While you are putting in your money each day, you can add to the magic by waving your two-dollar magic wand, tapping it on the lid of the box, and saying out loud, "I am richer today than I was yesterday!" (If you make it a family game, you can do it together and say, "We are richer today than we were yesterday!") Every day, you will be planting new seeds of financial success and prosperity in your subconscious mind(s). You'll be delighted to see how these seeds will take root and grow.

The second way money gets into this box is if you save some money using any of the other ideas in this book. Maybe you've spent less by doing price comparisons, by buying in bulk, by clipping coupons, by buying clothes in off-season clearances, by waiting for sales to make big purchases, or by negotiating a lower price. As soon as you get home, take out your purse or wallet and remove exactly the amount of money you saved. Walk right over to the magic box and put the money in. (Wave your hand or your magic wand: "I am richer today than I was yesterday!") Remember, if you hadn't made a conscious decision to be frugal, this money would have been *spent*, not saved. Since it would have been gone anyway, pretend it really is gone and just put it in the box instead. You'll be amazed by how fast this money will add up.

The critical factor: *Money in the magic box can never be spent—only invested.* At some regular interval—once a week, once a month, etc.—take all the money in the box and put it into a special savings account. When the amount in the savings account gets large enough, move it into a higher-paying investment.

You'll soon see that I'm not kidding; this box truly produces magic. Try the idea for a month, and you'll see what I mean. This may well become one of your favorite games once you see how much fun it is and how fast the dollars add up for your investments. It's MAGIC!

## ACTION STEPS

1. Forget all the other games for now. (If you just master this game, your entire financial life will do a 180-degree turn for the better.)

2. Find a box and a magic wand (a stick from the yard will do) and practice your magical phrases (see above).

3. Put some amount of money into the box each day, wave your magic wand over the box, and repeat the mantra: "I'm richer today than I was yesterday."

4. Read all the other games and start saving bucketloads[16] of money. Make sure your bucket is a giant one! We're going to a gold mine; take the biggest bucket you can find.

5. Put all the money you save from the other games into the magic box as well.

---

[16] "Bucketload" is a synonym for "chunk." It also means "a lot more than a little, but less than a zillion."

6. Remember the critical ingredient in the magical recipe: the money in the box can never be spent.

7. As soon as you have a significant sum in the box, put it into an interest-bearing savings account.

8. When the savings in that account grow large enough, move the money into a higher-paying investment.

9. E-mail me a picture of yourself wearing your look of "Wow! I'm so happy! This is great!!"

10. Buy copies of this book for all your friends so they can "experience the magic" as well.[17]

---

[17] There's one exception: don't buy the book for anyone who lives on your block. If you want to be "the millionaire next door to a bunch of broke folks," you'll need to jealously guard your secrets.

# Time Travel

## H. G. Wells will be jealous!

### Traveling to the Past

Do you have any anxieties, worries, or cares that are currently troubling you? Here's a great way to use "time travel" to improve your current situation. Get comfortable, relax any tension in your body, close your eyes, and using your marvelous mind, travel back in time six months.

Think about what your situation was like at that time and reflect on everything you could have started doing then that would have made your life today more peaceful, serene, and carefree. Then open your eyes and write down everything that occurred to you.

Congratulations! Through the miracle of time travel, you've just created a resource list that can help enhance your present and your future. Consider your list carefully. Implement any of the ideas you wish you'd thought of six months ago. It's never too late to do the right thing.

### Traveling in the Present

Start something. All of us have projects or tasks that we keep delaying because we dread them or hope they'll go away if we ignore them. Amazingly, nearly every task is easier in reality than we believe it will be before we start doing it.

So what are you waiting for? List your projects, pick one, and get moving. It doesn't really matter which one; starting *any* one will get you feeling more positive and productive. Since this is a book about money, why not pick one that will increase your financial education, reduce your debt, or produce some extra income? No matter which one you pick, you win!

And now that you've started, finish something. Let's add to the list of projects. So far, you've listed the new projects you hadn't started. The next step to improving your present situation is to add all your half-finished projects to the list. Did you start to balance your checkbook but give up halfway? Did you start reading a financial book (maybe this one!) and set it aside before finishing it? Did you start to research a new financial topic like no-load mutual funds or DRIPs (Dividend Reinvestment Plans) but set your materials aside midstream? Did you intend to go to the bank to set up a separate savings account to use as an emergency fund but put it off until later? Did you buy some financial software like Quicken but never install it? Did you read and like the ideas in some of these money games, but you just haven't taken the steps to try them?

If you have a great project that will help improve your financial position and you just haven't ever finished it, now is the time. There's no joy quite like that of a finished project.

## Traveling to the Future

Wow! What could be more fun (or scary) than getting a glimpse of things to come? Don't worry—since this is a game, we're only going to travel to a future filled with fun, excitement, accomplishments, and abundant wealth!

Here's how to travel. As when you traveled back in time, get comfortable, relax any tension in your body, and close your eyes. Now, using your marvelous mind, travel … but this time, travel forward ten years.

Now that you have arrived ten years in the future, describe your life exactly as you'd like it to be at that time. If all your dreams came true and then some, what would your life be like? How many residences would you have, and where would they be? What would you be wearing? What would you be doing for income, for entertainment, for travel, for leaving a legacy? What would you be driving? Would a chauffeur be driving you? How many vehicles would you own? Would any of them be boats or airplanes? Would you own a flying car or a helicopter? How much wealth would you have? (Name the specific dollar amount of your new net worth and specify how it is all invested.) How would you be spending your money? Would you be using your great wealth to help others? If so, how?

Picture every detail of your future: the color of the car, the smell of the saltwater from your beachfront home, the smell of the pines at your secluded cabin, the sun rising over the ocean from your forty-foot yacht, the people around you, and that specific, giant number that is your future net worth. Use all your senses, and describe in writing exactly what you would see, hear, taste, touch, and smell. Once you've written down *everything* about your perfect future, the most amazing part of this game begins.

Imagine it is still ten years in the future. The phone is ringing, and when you answer, an editor from *People Magazine* is on the other end. You can't believe what she is saying. "We've heard about your amazing success story—how you've completely changed your life for the better over the last ten years. We'd like to have you write a story for our readers titled 'How I Did It.' We think your story is so inspiring that we want all our readers to learn about you and the amazing things you did. We're willing to pay you $150,000 for the story. Will you write it for us?" she asks.

"Make it $200,000, and you've got a deal," you reply.

"Consider it a contract. How soon can we expect to receive your article?"

You hang up the phone, still amazed at the offer but jumping up and down with enthusiasm at the prospect of writing the article. You are so inspired that you get up right that minute to start writing.

So now, in reality, get out a yellow legal pad or your laptop and actually start your article: "How I Did It," by (insert your name here). Describe every step you took from that fateful day ten years earlier until the present day ten years later. You will find this to be an amazing exercise! Writing your "How I Did It" story from the perspective of looking back is guaranteed to be very revealing for you.

Finally, mentally compare what you said you did in your essay with what you are really doing now. What's different? Start changing your present actions to match the ones you looked back on from the future, and your future is guaranteed change for the better!

## ACTION STEPS

1. Look back six months and evaluate what you could have done then to make your life better now. Start implementing those changes now so that your life will be better in another six months.

2. Find present-day projects that you dream about but haven't started. Get one started.

3. List present-day projects you have started but haven't finished. If you have some partial projects hanging around that you'll likely never go back to, get rid of the "evidence." Throw them out or give them away. Then, from the remaining, partially completed projects, pick the one that's tugging at your heart most. Pull the cord and start it up again.

4. Imagine your perfect life ten years in the future. Write an essay titled "How I Did It," describing everything you did over the next ten years that led to that wonderful future you pictured in your mind. Compare what you are really doing today with what your essay said you did. Then start aligning your present actions to match those that led to your dreams coming true.

# MUSICAL GAMES

# Fanfare

## Programming your brain for success.

You may have read or heard about some of the studies connecting music to learning and enhancing performance. Researchers have found that music helps to improve cognitive functions—that is, it helps people to achieve better mental performance. Researchers also believe that different music has different effects on the brain. It may be that each of us tends to choose particular music based on our predominant emotions at specific times. Although they cannot say what music fits best in every specific situation, there seems to be agreement that music—even background music—provides a positive learning environment.

"Fanfare" is a game that came out of the reading I did about these studies. If music can provide a positive learning environment, it seemed logical to try to connect music to my attempts to improve my financial situation.

Here's the game: Decide what kind of music gets you really pumped up and excited. I call this "fanfare music." I made a collection of music that I associated with success. My playlist included music like the theme from *Rocky*, the theme from *Superman*, and *The Olympic Theme*. Assemble your own collection of music. It doesn't matter whether you have a stack of CDs, burn a new CD, or assemble songs on your MP3 player. Just have the music readily available.

Next, watch for positive events related to your money:

- making an extra or larger-than-normal payment on a credit card or loan;
- paying off a credit card or loan;
- starting a new investment;
- putting money into your Magic Box;
- saving a chunk or a bucketload of money using any of the games;
- seeing your net worth increase.

As soon as you note something good happening with your money, immediately get out your "pumped up and excited" music, play it nice and loud, jump and dance around, and just generally whoop it up. I can't prove the association, but the more I played the music, the more excited I got about playing it again. The music became my victory dance music as related to my money. Everything started to go better.

This game really got me excited about my money and about seeing my finances improve. It may sound hokey, but trust me, it's worth a try!

ACTION STEPS

1. Assemble your "fanfare music."
2. Watch for positive experiences with your money.
3. Play the music every time something fiscally exciting happens. If you are richer now than you were yesterday, play the music. Jump up, dance, and whoop it up. You are on the road to wealth!

PS: Also see the "Quick Hit" game "Chimes." You'll encounter the same idea, but it takes this sound-based game and moves it into the arena of the smelly!

# Trombone

### You'll want some very dark sunglasses–
### this one's outrageous!

The idea for this game comes from the wonderful audio series *Prosperity Consciousness,* by Fredric Lehrman.[18] While I haven't personally tried this wild idea, it sounds like so much fun that I just might. If you try it, please write and let me know how it goes. Here's how to play:

**Step 1:** Gather your props. You will need:

- a chair to sit in;
- a large piece of poster board and some markers;
- a large, empty coffee can or an old top hat;
- a musical instrument of some kind—a kind you *don't* know how to play, not even a little. A trombone might be nice. A noisy instrument is best. Borrow one from a local band member you know.

**Step 2:** Find a nice, public corner in your town where street performers (musicians, magicians, etc.) occasionally hang out or where you think they *should* hang out. Make sure it's a high-traffic area. Foot traffic, that is—not automobiles. You may want a costume of some kind and some very dark sunglasses, as you may not want to be recognized. In fact, you may want a corner in some *other* town, preferably a town where no one knows you!

**Step 3:** Decide how much money per hour you need to earn. Let's say it's $12. Take all your props to your public spot at a time when there are likely to be lots of people. Set up your chair, your coffee can or top hat (for donations), and your large sign, which should read something like, "I need to make $12 per hour. If I do not earn this much, I will play the trombone."

Yes, I realize you *can't* play the trombone. That's the whole point. You will sound pretty awful when you try to. So awful, in fact, that people will laugh and contribute to your hourly fund just to get you to stop! Good luck—or as our *Star Wars* friends might say, "May the Farce be with you."

---

[18]   http://www.nightingale.com/prod_detail~product~Prosperity_Consciousness.aspx

ACTION STEPS

1. Find some very dark sunglasses.
2. Borrow a trombone or other loud musical instrument you have no clue how to play.
3. Gather up a chair and any other props you want, including a sign (as per above).
4. Travel to a nearby town where no one knows you.
5. See how much really obnoxious noise you can make.
6. Gather in bucketloads of money and laugh all the way to the bank.

# QUICK HIT GAMES

# Another Dam(n) Game

## Put a giant smile on your face. You'll be living large!

When we put a dam on a river or stream, the water starts backing up and accumulating until the space set aside to store it reaches capacity. In this game, you are to set up a savings account that money can likewise only flow into until it is "full."

What happens when a reservoir becomes full? The excess either spills over the dam and is wasted or is released deliberately and thoughtfully—to generate hydroelectric power, for example. Just as with a real-life dam, the dam you set up for your money is designed to accumulate money up to whatever level you decide.

How much of your income should you retain in the reservoir behind your dam? You should try for a minimum of 10 percent, but if you are still trying to pay off debts or are still learning to live within your means, 5, 3, or even 1 percent may be acceptable. Boost the percentage when you can.

Dams can generate enormous amounts of power. (Research Hoover Dam if it interests you.) Your financial dams can generate enormous "power" too. The amounts will be small in the beginning, but as the money accumulates, it will amaze and delight you how much income (power) your money will generate for you while you are doing other things.

Once the money in your savings account has reached your predetermined limit, take the extra money and invest it in other places that have the potential to earn higher returns. (You might think of this as building additional dams. They, too, will only accumulate money.) Many years and many dams from now, when you reach retirement age, you will begin the process of letting the "overflow," or earnings, from these financial dams flow into your life to augment your other retirement income.

Imagine if your combined dams accumulate $1,000,000, or $2,000,000, or $6,000,000, or more! If you move the money to a safe and secure place like U.S. Treasury bills or bonds, for example, and make even a 4 percent return, you can add $40,000, $80,000, or $240,000 to your retirement income without even touching the principal. That's spectacular!

ACTION STEPS

1. Build financial dams—lots of them, and big ones!
2. Let the money accumulate until you retire.
3. Put a giant smile on your face. You'll be living large.

# Barbecue

## Fifteen minutes a day is all I ask.

I can make an outrageous hamburger on our outdoor, built-in grill in fourteen minutes. Seven minutes per side on high heat, and I have the perfect burger. Now, it's true that the grill does have to warm up and get up to its maximum heat level, but once it's warmed up, I can make perfect burgers one after the other in very short time periods.

Try this: Cook with your financial barbecue for the same amount of time each day—let's round it up to fifteen minutes to make it easier to track on the clock. Remember, as with the outdoor grill, you'll need to give your financial barbecue time to get hot before you can use it efficiently. In this case, that means setting financial goals. Once your goals are in place, spend just fifteen minutes per day planning, reviewing, tracking, thinking, and studying anything related to your financial "burger," and you'll soon be the envy of the neighborhood when it comes to financial success.

What you think about is attracted into your life. Once you see what amazing results you'll get from spending just fifteen minutes a day on your finances, you'll be eager to increase the time you spend on this activity.

Prove me right on this one. Try it. If you don't find yourself moving much more quickly toward your financial goals than you were before, I'll cook you up a burger. No, I'm not stocking my refrigerator. I know this works.

ACTION STEPS

1. Set your financial goals.

2. Agree to devote fifteen minutes per day to your financial life. Try seven minutes per side—seven minutes tracking and reviewing and seven minutes thinking and studying—and you'll still have an entire minute left to spend picturing the perfect future your money will let you create.

3. E-mail me in amazement. You truly won't believe what fifteen minutes a day will do for your financial success!

# Chimes ("Smelling" Your Way to Success)

**It starts innocently on the patio, but then it starts getting smelly.**

We've already talked about the link between music and success, but what about other sounds? I believe they can also have a connection if you intend them to. Picture this scene: I have a favorite chair on the back patio where I like to relax and meditate. From the chair, I can hear two backyard fountains and a small set of hanging wind chimes close by. Over time, this combination of sounds and the fact that I often think and pray and meditate in that area have combined to help me quickly achieve an alpha state (quiet mind) nearly as soon as I sit down. Whenever I'm in that spot, I try to spend some time reviewing my past successes and visualizing future positive outcomes.

Unfortunately, I can't carry that environment with me wherever I go, and I can't spend all my time there. However, I do use it at least once a week as a place to relax and meditate, so my mind and body just naturally associate those sounds with success.

I can also hear those same wind chimes and fountains from my family room and my master bedroom. It didn't connect for me at first, but I found myself winding down and feeling relaxed in those rooms whenever the windows were open. It seems like those sounds have connected with relaxation in my mind. Even if I'm not on my patio, hearing the sounds I associate with relaxation allows me to relax in other places.

The "aha" moment when I realized that connection caused me to wonder how I could use sound to help me in other away-from-home situations. This may seem strange, but I decided to experiment and create a CD with "success music" on it that I could listen to almost anywhere I went. (You may remember this from the prior musical game "Fanfare.")

Every piece of music I associated with success went on that CD. At first, I only listened to the CD *after* I had just experienced some type of success, adding to the positive euphoria of the moment.

After some time, I also started listening to the CD when I was practicing for some future success I wanted to achieve, like when I was studying for an insurance exam. When I would go to sit for the exam, I would sit in my car in the parking lot with my eyes closed and listen to the CD first. Then after successfully passing the exam—which I've done every time since!—I would listen to the CD again in the car right afterward.

Are you ready to take this whole process to yet another level? Be warned: this is where things start getting "smelly." Read on …

When I related this process to one of my friends (yep, that's you, Commander), he told me that he does something very similar, but with smell! While studying, he would burn a certain fragrance of candle. Then, before he went to take his exams, he would scratch one of the candles to get a bit of the wax underneath his fingernails. During the exam, all he had to do was have one hand near his nose, and the "scent of success" was right with him.

I haven't tried his technique yet, but I'm certain to do so. After hearing my way to success with sound, smelling my way to even greater success sounds like it's worth a try!

## ACTION STEPS

1. Every time you have a success, listen to the same music or arrange to smell the same fragrance. Do this enough times to establish a mental link between your successes and the sounds and/or smells.

2. Once a mental link is in place, you are ready to start using this technique in a proactive manner. Do you have a future success that you are preparing for or visualizing? You can start listening to your music and/or smelling your fragrance while you are readying yourself for your next success. Your successes will multiply quite amazingly.

# Composting

## Some rottin' advice.

Let me just say this right now—I'm no gardener! The extent of my knowledge of composting is about the same as, say, my knowledge of outer Mongolia: miniscule. Lack of knowledge hasn't hindered me thus far, however, so we'll just pretend my thumbs are as green as can be and move right along.

If you are a gardener, you will probably cringe at this description, but as I understand it, composting is taking a bunch of garbage and manure, dumping them in a deep hole, covering them, and letting them "rot real good" for some unspecified period of time. That sounds pretty boring. However, I've also been told that after the aforesaid unspecified period of time, that same compost can be dug up (eww!) and used as magnificent fertilizer for plants and whatever else one grows in a garden. (I hereby render my apologies to my long-departed grandparents, who were prize-winning gardeners. I'm sure I've completely humiliated our family name.)

However, in order to partially redeem my status as a family member, I would like to offer this humble saying, which might help anyone reading this chapter (you're still *with* me?) to improve his or her financial lot in life: "good things can come from bad things." If dinner scrapings, orange peels, apple cores, manure, and other detritus can be mixed together, allowed to ferment, and then used as exceptional fertilizer, then just think what good can come from all the financial mistakes you've made, are making, and will make in the future!

Let's face it. We've all made numerous and sometimes sizeable financial blunders. If I had started saving and investing at age sixteen, when I got my first job, rather than waiting until I was twenty-five, my current net worth would likely be north of $5,000,000, and I'd be long gone from the working world. Dang—that mistake cost me! But the point is, what have I learned from my various mistakes?

At age twenty-five, I realized the value of saving money and letting it compound over time. Even though I was late, I started moving in the right direction right away. That was good.

At age forty, I realized that I should have started maximizing my 401(k) when I first started it about thirteen years earlier. That was bad. How did I respond? I immediately started maximizing it! That was good.

Once I bought Enron stock, and it started going down in value. That was bad. But once I realized that Enron stock was useless, I got rid of it. That was good.

Yes, I could go on and on, but I'm sure you get the point. A mistake is never fatal if we learn from it, correct our courses, and move forward. I've made mistakes. You've made mistakes. Let's pile them all together and make some compost. If we are smart and learn from each other's mistakes as well as our own, those mistakes can be just the fertilizer we need to grow a prize-winning financial fortune. They may be a little "smelly," but they'll have great value to us if we let them propel us forward with greater knowledge and enthusiasm.

Got any spare apple cores you don't need?

## ACTION STEPS

1. Realize that no financial mistake is ever fatal if you are willing to learn from it and use it to improve what you do from then on.

2. Know that you can't possibly make every single financial mistake on your own. (You'll be lucky if you can make a couple hundred or so.)

3. Realize that many financial wizards have made egregious financial mistakes. The good news is that they've left books behind that explain what they did wrong and how they corrected their mistakes and moved on to wealth.

4. Those books are available to us to learn from, and they're free at the local library! What are we waiting for? We need to do some composting!

# Generator/Alternator

## It's a powerful question to help you generate better alternatives and make better choices.

Surprise—this game doesn't have much of anything to do with cars! Instead, it is about learning to spend your money on things that will generate value in your life and learning that you always have alternate choices when you make spending decisions.

My favorite definition of money is that it is an exchange of energy—your life energy. As we spend our time and life energy for others, we are rewarded with money (something tangible) that we can use to trade for items produced by the time and life energy of others. Most people realize the wisdom of using their money to cover their basic needs (food, housing, medical care, insurance, etc.) before spending money to upgrade their standards of living (buying a new car, a nicer home, etc.). What we don't always remember is that we also have the choice to take an intermediate step between meeting our basic needs and trying to fulfill our wants and desires.

Think this through: When you *spend* money, someone is on the opposite side of that same transaction making a financial profit. So if you are making a decision to spend some of your money, why not learn to do so in ways that will bring profit to your own life? For example, you might choose to spend money on things that will add to your knowledge or enhance your skills. What is the likely result if you buy and read a book on your industry? Your job performance will improve, and you will have a good chance of receiving a higher salary and accumulating more money to spend later!

Why shouldn't you profit from the use of your money as well as the earning of your money? Sometimes your best investment is in investing in yourself! A powerful question for you to ask yourself before any expenditure is, "Are there any better uses for this money?"

ACTION STEPS

1. Spend your life energy helping others and receive an income for your efforts.

2. After meeting your basic survival needs, pause to carefully consider what you will do with the *next* portion of your income.

a.   Most people will immediately head for the "nice to have" aisles of their favorite stores and load up on discretionary items. Why not consider using at least a small portion of your income on things that will add to your knowledge and/or enhance your skills?

b.   You are an income "generator." You can be an "alternator" as well if you carefully choose how to use the income you have generated. You always have alternate choices.

3.   Always ask yourself, "Are there any better uses for this money?"

# RASKLE

**How recognizing the sound of a "skooch" and listening to thunder can make you millions.**

I admit it—I'm a rascal and proud of it! Better yet, though, is my internal RASKLE. That's my acronym for my Reticular Activating System. My RASKLE brought me a million dollars! (Actually, "he" is just finishing bringing me my *second* million dollars.) Now, that's a RASKLE you can love.

So what exactly is the Reticular Activating System? As it has been described to me, it is a part of your brain that acts like a filtering system. Thank goodness we have them. Think of all the sensory bombardments that surround us all the time. If we were continuously conscious of all of them, we'd probably go insane.

Stop and take note of what each of your senses is telling you right now. At the moment, I hear thunder (cool!), a lawn mower, a ceiling fan, the refrigerator, the hum of my laptop, the sound of my fingers on the keyboard, the "skooch" of my bare feet on the coffee table, a car driving by, and the wind in the trees outside the window.

I am now aware of nine things, and I was only paying attention to my sense of hearing. It would take paragraphs and paragraphs more to add what all my other senses are adding to the mix. Was I actually consciously aware of all those sounds before I started paying attention? No, not until I chose to focus on them. Were they there all along? Yes. My RASKLE was just filtering them out for me because they weren't important. (All but the thunder, that is—I love thunder.)

The most amazing job RASKLE ever did for me was to filter out the smell of more than 100,000 cattle's worth of cow pies warming up after a rainstorm. You see, I used to live in a town where there were feedlots to the north of town, and the prevailing wind was from the north! The cows actually outnumbered the city residents by about six to one. It was great for the local economy but rough on the olfactory system, at least in the beginning. After some months of living in the area, I had a visitor from out of state come to see me. He said "Wow—how can you live with that *smell* all the time?" I actually found myself replying truthfully, "What smell?" RASKLE had actually learned to filter out that smell for me, and I didn't even notice it until someone pointed it out. How marvelous is that?!

Now, the other interesting thing about RASKLE is that he also filters *in* things that I *do* want to be aware of—things that I am focusing on. For instance, at age

twenty-five, I set a goal of being a millionaire by age sixty-five, starting with a whopping net worth of $1,500, including my socks. I focused on that goal deliberately for an hour at least once a week; quite often, I did it *daily!* So RASKLE set to work on what I was focusing on so intently and brought me all kinds of ideas (like many in this book) on how to save, where to invest, how to decrease my debts, and how to take other actions to move me toward my goal.

RASKLE did such a great job of listening to what I wanted that he actually helped me achieve the goal fifteen years ahead of schedule! Now that I've realized what a good job he does, I've given him a much bigger goal—*much* bigger!

Are you wondering how I came up with the name RASKLE for him? It is an acronym for Reticular Activating System (K)an Lead to Enormity! (Sorry, I know that was painful—but it's still a cute name.)

What you focus on intently tends to be attracted to you. What work are you giving *your* RASKLE?

## ACTION STEPS

1. Learn about your Reticular Activating System.
2. Decide what goals you'd really like to achieve.
3. Focus on those goals with all the intensity and frequency you can muster.
4. Let RASKLE do the rest.

# Shopping

## You have my permission to quote me on this.

As far as I know, Americans are the world's best consumers. (No, I can't say I'm especially proud of that.) What do consumers do? Duh—they consume! That is, they use things up. The exact number escapes me, but I recently read that Americans consume a hugely disproportionate share of the world's resources. That bummed me out, and I'm trying—in my own tiny way—to lessen that statistic.

Nevertheless, there is a truism I just made up (can I do that?) that goes like this: "Savers will always be wealthy; consumers will always be poor." You have my permission to quote me on that.

Why will consumers always be poor in relation to savers? Let's look at what they do. When the supermarket has a sale on, say, toilet paper, the consumer runs in and stocks up. Sadly, at least in one way, I am a testament to that. If we ever have the big one in southern California (earthquake, that is), the one thing I definitely won't run out of is toilet paper. I have so much that I'll be able to sell it to the neighbors on the black market.

To summarize, if something is on sale, the consumer snaps it up. Conversely, if the supermarket raises its prices, the consumer shops elsewhere.

Oddly, there is one circumstance under which the consumer gets completely confused and acts contrary to his/her nature. When the stock market has a sale, most often called a crash or correction, the consumer runs away from it. But when the stock market raises its prices, the consumer starts buying. Explain that one to me, will you please? I just don't get it.

Savers, on the other hand, are obviously always on the lookout for ways to save. Now, that sounds similar on the surface, but it really isn't. Savers want to *hold on to* their money, not let it go to the retailer of the month. A saver may join the consumer at the T.P. sales, but only with the idea in mind that they will save money in the future. Sales eventually end, and the price of T.P. will no doubt rise again. Since the saver now has a more-than-sufficient supply on hand, he will not need to buy any of the higher-priced T.P., and that will free up extra money for him to put into investments. The saver will be *adding* to the household income, not taking away from it.

The saver will also always try to buy stock when it's "on sale"—after a crash, a big downturn, etc. Crashes tend to worry the average Joe and Josie, and they'll run away. Mr./Ms. Saver, on the other hand, is eager to buy exactly what no one else wants because that's when it's available at the lowest price. Joe and Josie Consumer wait until *everyone* (even their hairdresser) is excited about a stock or investment to buy. And by then, because the demand is so high, the price is as well. The Savers are thrilled to sell to them.

You've heard this rule before, but it is rarely practiced by the typical consumer in the stock market: buy low, sell high. Buy it when no one else will touch it with a ten-foot pole, and sell it when the world and our six closest neighboring planets are clamoring for it.

## ACTION STEPS

1. Remember that there are a few billion other inhabitants of this planet and try not to use more than your share of the resources.

2. Take your after-Christmas-sale enthusiasm and direct it toward items that will grow in value rather than depreciate.

3. Take the best advice of the frenzied crowds and do your best to do just the opposite. If they buy, you sell. If they sell, you buy.

4. Call me from your yacht in twenty years. I'll sail up to meet you, and we'll go shopping!

# Sunshine on Your Shoulder

## All I really wanted was a nap!

Have you ever heard of writer's block? It's a strange phenomenon that occasionally happens to writers where they just suddenly run out of breath, so to speak, and get stuck on whatever they are writing. Their minds go completely blank, their pulses rise, and they begin to sweat.

At least that's what happened to me recently. I was just merrily writing along in this book, chapter by chapter, and all of a sudden I just completely ran out of ideas for any more games. Now, that might not seem like cause for concern, but at that moment I had only written enough games to fill about two-thirds of this book. That wasn't good. I sat with my laptop for the longest time, but it was just no use. There just weren't any more ideas coming out.

That's when I accidentally discovered the game that I'm about to describe to you. I set the laptop aside in frustration and headed down to the back patio to sit in my lounge chair where I think and meditate. Though to be honest, thinking and meditating were not even on my mind at that moment. What was really on my mind was a nice nap in the sunshine. I took a book with me just to give any passersby the impression that I was being productive, but the real goal was to sleep.

Now, if you have read the chapter titled "Chimes," you'll know that this lounge chair is also my "success" chair. When I'm there, I am surrounded by relaxing sounds and sights, so I am accustomed to doing my thinking and meditating in that spot. Not that it mattered—I was after a *nap!!*

So I began the process of napping. I closed my eyes, let my muscles relax, emptied my mind—though there was nothing in it anyway, due to my writer's block—and I was just about to doze off when what did I hear? Chimes!

Hey, "Chimes!" That would make a great title and idea for a money game. Grabbing a pen I'd brought out with my book, I opened the book to an empty page at the back and quickly jotted down the word "chimes." I knew I'd remember later what my concept was.

I went back to dozing. Oops! There was the sound of the hummingbirds nearby, wrangling over the food supply I'd put out for them. Well, I'll be. "Hummingbirds" would be a great chapter too! Quickly, I opened my eyes again and jotted down the second title.

That's enough. Let's sleep. Sadly, at least from the napping perspective, every time I shut my eyes, another idea for a money game would pop into my head. I thought of nine new ideas in the space of twenty-five minutes. Then I leaned back to relax again, and I was just about asleep when I thought, "Wow, that sunshine on my shoulder really feels great."

Yes, at that moment, the real revelation hit me, along with the title for *this* "game." Sometimes the best thing we can do to move a project forward is to get away from it, do something completely different, and relax. It gives RASKLE (see his game) time to work unhindered.

So the next time you are stuck, perplexed, flummoxed, concerned, anxious, or at a loss as to how to move forward, look for some sunshine. If you can angle yourself so the sun hits your shoulder, all the better.

## ACTION STEPS

1.  If you are "stuck" with something related to your finances (or some other part of your life), sometimes the best thing to do is to just tell your RASKLE what it is you want and then let go of it for a while.

2.  In the meantime, you can always head for some sunshine. Make sure it hits your shoulder.

# Write On!

## It's true–the first year really felt pitiful.

As you consider many of the games in this book, you will find many ideas floating around in your head. You will also receive many assignments and tasks, should you choose to accept them, that require (you guessed it!) something to write on.

In the early days of my financial life, I didn't have a personal computer because they didn't exist yet. All I had was a pile of notebook paper, some pens and markers, a handheld calculator, and many, many ideas. Our wealth started to grow pretty slowly, and it initially felt pretty darn pitiful. (We had only saved $600 by the end of the first year! It was hard to believe we'd get rich at that rate.)

However, the numbers eventually started getting larger, and pretty soon I needed to set up a way to keep track of the assorted papers that were accumulating. I had my list of goals, a spreadsheet that tracked our net worth, our monthly budget, and the statements we were receiving from the Credit Union.

My initial solution was a bright red, three-ring binder filled with lots of notebook paper and accounting ledger paper. Thus began my Money Journal. Over the years, it has morphed many times. It has expanded, shrunk, changed over to computer and back, then back again, but I can guarantee that I'll always have one.

Regardless of what you put in yours, how often you update it, or how diligent you are about keeping up with it, I highly recommend that you start your own Money Journal.[19] Something magical happens once you commit your goals and dreams to paper. They seem to take on a life of their own, and your progress snowballs and gains energy and speed. There is great power in seeing your goals in print, in physically tracking your progress against those goals, and in having something you can hold in your hand that represents your most amazing dreams.

Make a fancy cover if you want. Add pictures and drawings of your dream home, your dream cars, and your dream yacht—everything you can think of that represents your ideal future. My binder has also included mind maps at times. (Do an Internet search or ask about books on that topic at your local library

---

[19] If you would like one already printed and ready to go so you can literally just "fill in the blanks" each day, look for a book by Yvonne Brooks called *Daily Financial Journal: Spiritual Leadership Series Volume Two.* New York: iUniverse, Inc., 2006. Every time I've used it consistently, my finances have improved.

or bookstore if you aren't familiar with this organizing and brainstorming technique—it's powerful.)

To this day, I still love opening that old, red, three-ring binder, which I still have. Yes, I have most of its contents on computer these days, but there's still something special about that binder. It's traveled with me from rags to riches and been a constant source of encouragement and excitement over twenty-eight years.

If you are the primary "money person" in your household (the retentive one who makes all the spreadsheets, does all the tracking, etc.), then the binder has yet another useful purpose: it can be the main source of financial information for your spouse or significant other if something happens to you.

## ACTION STEPS

1. Have a central location or binder in which to keep all the records of your financial journey.

2. Include pictures, sketches, drawings, and photos of anything related to your future dreams.

3. Track your progress frequently (at least monthly). I tracked weekly, and although that's over the top, I know it kept my goals firmly in front of RASKLE. If my weekly review helped me reach my first milestone goal fifteen years sooner than I had planned, it was well worth it!

# SAVINGS GAMES

# 10-10-10

## Poor people spend first and save what's left. Rich people ...

True wealth builders rarely live on more than 70 percent of their take-home pay. What happens to the other 30 percent? They divide it up as follows: 10 percent off the top goes to charity. Ten percent goes to debt reduction as long as any debt remains, and 10 percent goes to saving and/or investing. When all the debts are paid off, that 10 percent for reducing debt can go toward increased saving or be invested in a personal business or hobby that brings additional income.

If you can gradually learn to live on 70 percent or less of your take-home income, you can easily become wealthy. Yes, yes, I hear you: "But I can't even live on 100 percent, let alone a smaller percentage!" If that's true for you, remember that you don't have to start with 10-10-10. You may need to start out with 1-1-1 in the beginning and gradually build up your savings and investments from there. That's okay. It's more important that you get used to the practice than how large your percentages are.

Rich people have different habits than most of the population. As someone once said, "Poor people spend first and save what's left; rich people save first and spend what's left." That's good information to know! Just set a target and gradually increase your goals in the nonspending categories. As your expenses decrease—these games will help with that—and your income increases, you can easily increase the percentages that go to charity, debt reduction, and savings.

Remember: It doesn't matter where you start as long as you are moving in the right direction. Take note, however: *None of the numbers can be zero.*[20] At least 1 percent of your income must go to charity, 1 percent must go to debt reduction, and 1 percent must go to saving and investing.

Feel free to tinker with the percentages to fit your situation. As a general guideline, I like the thought of increasing the percentage that goes to debt if your debts have interest rates higher than 8 or 9 percent. If the interest rates on your debts are lower than that and your investments are earning higher rates of return, you can consider putting the higher percentage of your income in investments instead.

---

[20] Okay, so there is one exception. Once you are completely debt-free, the debt reduction number can be zero!

Remember that distinction between poor people and rich people. *Rich people save first.* You can have all the fun you want with the portion of your money that is left. Eat, drink, and be merry, for today you set aside the money that will provide you with a happier tomorrow.

## ACTION STEPS

1. Take these life-changing words to heart: "Poor people spend first and save what's left; rich people save first and spend what's left."

2. Start small if necessary, but work toward living on 70 percent of your take-home pay.

3. Devote 10 percent of your income to charity, 10 percent to reducing your debt, and 10 percent to building your savings and investing.

4. When your debts are paid off, use that 10 percent toward either of the other categories or to start a personal business or hobby that brings in additional income.

# Breathing

## At least I admit it when I'm odd.

You want to continue living, right? What's necessary for that to happen? You must continue breathing. For this game, from this day forward, you are going to think about money every time you become conscious of your breathing.

Okay, yes, that's odd. But at least I admit it when I'm odd. (My psychiatrist can vouch for that.) Think about breathing for a minute. What has to happen in order for breathing to be successful? There must be both inflow and outflow. What would happen if you only took air in and never let any out? Well, you'd *die*, that's what! To live, you must both take in air and expel air.

Try this: Take in fresh air, let your lungs enjoy and make use of the oxygen, and then let out the carbon dioxide that remains and make room for more fresh air. Wasn't that wonderful? You can do it all day if you want to. Now take that same principle and apply it to money. In order for money to "be alive" and grow, it must have an inflow and an outflow as well. Let's be clear, however; "outflow" doesn't refer to spending your money at the mall.

My personal belief is that you should give the first portion of your income to your church or favorite charity before you spend the remainder for any other reason. Contributions to charity seem to have an interesting impact on monetary success. Why should you give away the first portion? If you spend all your money on your life first, you'll often find that there is nothing left over to give. Give first, and the rest will somehow work out just fine.

I'm not aware of any formal studies on this topic, but my informal observations tell me that overall, those who contribute to charity regularly are significantly more successful in the financial arena than those who don't.[21] In my experience, money has a tendency to flow *toward* those individuals who release a portion of it and *away* from those who hold it too tightly.

Consider this example in the natural world: The Red Sea is alive and flourishing with sea creatures. The Dead Sea will not support any marine life. The only

---

[21] See the book *The 9 Steps to Financial Freedom* (Orman 2006) for some similar observations. Also, be sure to look for "The Water Hose Game" in this book if you'd like a few further thoughts on this subject.

difference between the two is that the Red Sea has a natural *outflow* as well as inflow, and the Dead Sea has only inflow.

Because the Dead Sea is 1,300 feet below sea level at its shoreline, water is not able to drain out of it. Instead, water evaporates from it, leaving behind minerals that cause its salt content to increase. Fish and water plants are not able to live in it due to its high salinity. The flow of water in and out of other bodies of water such as the Red Sea prevents the buildup of such minerals and keeps salinity low enough to allow fish and plants to survive and thrive.

Is there a correlation between these two bodies of water and the success or failure of our personal finances? I believe there is. Inflow is good, but outflow is also necessary if we want financial health and well-being.

Don't take my word on this, however. Try it for yourself. Give a portion of your money to worthy causes. Do so for at least six months. I've looked into my "mental crystal ball," and I have a prediction for you. Your personal financial life will improve in direct proportion to the amount of money you release toward improving our world.

Start with 1 percent if you like. The initial percentage isn't as important as your attitude. Be thankful for the money you receive, and be happy that you can share part of it with others who may not be so fortunate. As your circumstances improve, continue increasing that percentage. Long term, I believe the percentage you give away should be at least 10 percent.[22]

## ACTION STEPS

1. Breathe in. Breathe out. Wasn't that wonderful? You can keep it up all day if you like.

2. Take in money. Give out money. Wasn't that wonderful too? You can keep it up your entire life if you like.

---

[22] This idea isn't limited to just money, either. You can also give your time and your possessions.

# Daily Double

## ... and me without a coupon in sight.

While we're on the subject of coupons (okay, so *pretend* we were), don't forget that there are supermarkets that let you play "daily double"—that is, they will double the value of any coupons you use toward your purchases. In fact, I was in Sedona, AZ, recently and wandered into a grocery store that paid *triple* value for coupons! A big smile spread across my face ... until I realized I was there without a single coupon. What a bummer.

Are coupons really worth all that trouble? Yes, *if* you can make a game out of collecting and using them. Coupons can definitely save you money, but bear these thoughts in mind:

Don't buy something just because you happen to have a coupon for it. Know the item's normal price, and compare that to its current price minus the coupon.

Check every shelf. The best deals are quite often on the hard to reach upper or lower shelves. You may have to reach up or bend down to get the best values. Even if you have a coupon, there may be better values in other sizes or quantities that you can get without coupons and/or better values in generics.

If you're really going to get into couponing, take advantage of the many resources available to you. Did you know that there are some great sites online where you can get free grocery coupons? If you tell these marketing companies what your favorite products are, they will give you cents-off coupons on many of those products! You give up some of your privacy as a consumer, but if you are using grocery store discount cards, you already have others tracking your purchases anyway. If you have Internet access and a printer, check out some of these sites[23]:

www.coolsavings.com

www.couponbug.com

www.couponcart.com

www.coupondispatch.com

---

[23] All these sites were active at the time I wrote this, but these sites change frequently. Try using any Internet search engine with "grocery coupon" in the search field. It's amazing what's out there!

www.couponorganizer.com

www.coupons.com

www.couponwinner.com

www.eversave.com

www.frugalshopper.com

www.happycoupons.com

www.hotcoupons.com/info/hcsc.htm

www.thecouponspot.com

www.thegrocerygame.com

www.valpak.com

Most of these sites require you to give up some of your personal information in return for the coupons, but hey, how many places know all about you already? (We won't go there.) If you aren't fond of giving out personal information, your best source for coupons will always be the Sunday newspaper. You can even have friends, neighbors, and family members save the inserts for you.

Another interesting way to get coupons is to call the toll-free phone numbers listed on many of your favorite brands and ask for coupons. If these companies have Web sites, you may find coupons there as well.

Still want more information? Here are two useful books:

- *Shop, Save, Share* (Kay 2002)
- *The Directory of Money Saving Coupons* (Gorchoff 2004)

Finally, check out www.shoppingkim.com. It's a great site for articles and links to other recommended resources.

Is it worth it? It takes time to search for, cut out, and organize coupons, not to mention weeding out expired coupons from the bunch. How many hours will it take you? Are there ways to spend those same hours in activities that have greater returns? Only you can decide.

## ACTION STEPS

1. Clip and use coupons, but only on items you would have bought anyway.

2. Research the many sources for coupons; there are a lot more available than you might realize.

3. Weigh the time expended vs. the dollars saved. Only you can decide if this game is worthwhile in your life.

# Double Daily Double

## I wish I had a dollar for every time
## I made one of these mistakes ...

Here's an offshoot of the coupon-using ideas—a sister game, so to speak—that I like to call "Double Daily Double." Sometimes an item will be offered at a sale price and also have a mail-in rebate that can save you even more! These offers are typically for higher-priced merchandise and usually exist to entice you to buy a particular brand among several competing brands.

Hewlett-Packard (HP) is a great example of this type of marketing. With sale prices and rebates, their printers are *free,* or nearly so! How can manufacturers afford to offer such good deals? Well, in the case of HP, it makes good financial sense in the long term to market the printers at low cost. Why? Because then you have to buy HP ink cartridges! Because their printers are reliable and last a long time, the company can make a large profit on the repeat sales of supplies. That's ingenious.

In addition, the manufacturers know that only a portion of the consumers will actually send in the rebate forms. I wish I had a dollar for every time I made one of the following mistakes:

- Procrastinating too long on mailing in the rebate form (i.e., until after the deadline has passed);

- Forgetting to keep the packaging with the necessary bar code you must send in with the receipt;

- Forgetting to even *keep* the receipt;

- Forgetting to get a rebate form from the merchant;

- Reading the instructions for the rebate, realizing I have to send in the original receipt, but needing a *copy* of the receipt for my tax records and thus setting aside the receipt until I can make a copy ... only to lose it or pass the rebate deadline.

Coupons and rebates are great—don't get me wrong. Some of us just don't have the patience and/or follow-through to make the best use of them. But if you can turn coupon- and rebate-collecting into a well-organized game with great follow-up, this is a game you will win!

## ACTION STEPS

1. Keep track of rebate offers.

2. Make sure you get the rebate information or coupon from the vendor.

3. Make copies of all receipts.

4. Keep all packaging until you have completed and mailed in the rebate. (You may need to send in bar codes or other information from the packaging in order to get your rebate.)

5. Keep track of rebate deadlines and be sure to send completed rebate forms and all required additional items well before those deadlines.

6. Send the author a note reminding him to follow his own advice.

# Escalator

## They're not fast, but they're always moving.

Wouldn't you love it if your financial life consistently grew and improved, constantly moving upward like an escalator? This is possible, all thanks to the "miracle" of pre-authorized checking account transactions. By signing a simple form and attaching a sample check from your checking account, there are multitudes of investments that you can set on autopilot.

Here are a few examples. You can

- set up your 401(k) to take an automatic, monthly deduction from your checking account;
- take automatic payroll deductions and have the money sent into credit unions or investment accounts;
- set up Dividend Reinvestment Plans (DRIPS)[24] that take automatic, monthly withdrawals from your account.

Escalators move continuously. Your investments should do the same. Taking that first step and consistently adding to your savings and investing accounts every month causes your financial position to move ever upward. Escalators don't move rapidly, but they are always progressing. Why not let your investments do the same?

ACTION STEPS

1. Set as many of your investments as possible on "autopilot" by adding money on a regular basis through pre-authorized checking account transactions.

2. Keep moving. Remember the escalator; it may move slowly, but it is constantly in motion and moves ever upward. That's your goal too!

---

[24] See the excellent book *The Individual Investor Revolution* (Carlson 2005) for a detailed description of DRIPs. DRIPs can help more of your savings money go directly into investments without the expense of a broker. Charles Carlson also edits an excellent newsletter on DRIPs with specific suggestions on companies worth considering. The newsletter is called *DRIP Investor* and is published by Horizon Publishing Company.

# Fast and Furious

**Here are fourteen things to do if your present financial condition is pretty pitiful, or at least somewhere less than optimal.**

Get mad, act quickly, score fast. Okay, so you don't really have to be "furious," but getting at least a little upset about your current financial status—assuming it's either pretty pitiful or somewhere less than optimal—isn't a bad thing. The less content you are with your current state of affairs, the more motivated you'll be to take action to improve things.

Does that sound like your situation? If so, you'll appreciate this chapter. The idea behind "Fast and Furious" is to get mad, act quickly, and score some quick victories. With that in mind, here's a list of easy things you can do starting today that will give you fast results and make you feel like you are making immediate progress toward a brighter financial future:

1.  Check the deductibles on your homeowner's, renter's, and auto insurance. If you can handle a little more of the "small stuff" yourself, raising your deductibles can save you plenty on your insurance costs.

2.  Drop premium channels from your cable or satellite TV service. Do you really need the John Wayne channel when you already have every one of his movies on DVD?

3.  Put clothes into the dryer for five minutes or less—just enough to get the wrinkles out—and then hang them to dry the rest of the way.

4.  Actually read the credit card offers that come to you in the mail. If you get an offer for a lower rate than you have on your current card, call your current card's office and tell them you've gotten an offer for a lower rate. Ask if they'll match it. If they say no, make the switch. Saving even 2 percent on your interest rate can make a difference.

5.  If possible, send in your credit card payments immediately when you receive the bills. The sooner the bank gets your payments, the less interest you will be charged.

6.  Pay cash rather than using credit cards. You'll find that you spend significantly less when you have to pay cash.

7. Consider walking or riding your bike as often as possible.

8. Pack a lunch and snacks for work. Drink water instead of buying sodas.

9. Read as many books as you can about finances and saving money, but get them from your local library. Did you know that most library cards are still free? Imagine that.

10. Avoid buying clothing that is dry clean only.

11. Avoid recreational shopping. If you don't have a necessary and specific purchase to make, what are you doing in that store?

12. Toss those catalogs. It's amazing what you didn't even know you needed but "just have to have" all of a sudden, now that you've seen it in a catalog.

13. Sell some stuff. If you are a true American, it's very likely that you have too much stuff. I've seen homes with three-car garages so full of excess stuff that the owners can't even park one car in them, let alone three. Get rid of that stuff!

14. Never give up. If you get in an accident, lose a job, suffer an illness, or have some other catastrophe that dumps you off the horse, get back on. Just start again. Remember: Get mad, act quickly, score fast.

## ACTION STEPS

1. Decide if your current financial status is pretty pitiful or somewhat less than optimal.

2. If your answer is "yes," look for ways to take quick actions that will start your finances moving in a more positive direction.

3. If these ideas appeal to you, see also the game "Machine Gun." You'll find an even longer list of possible finance-improving actions in that game.

# For Better or for Worse

## There are two roads here ...

Would you ever deliberately set yourself up to be financially worse off in the future? I doubt it. If you look at our culture, however, we've been taught to do exactly that. What does our marketplace tell us through advertising? "You can drive this Lexus and enjoy it every day *and* pay for it while you are enjoying it." Isn't that right? Moreover, your payments will only be $789 per month for six years. So, what's so bad about that? You can enjoy the Lexus and pay for it as you go. Well, maybe nothing is specifically bad about that, but you *are* making a decision to be worse off financially down the road.

Suppose you paid cash now for that car. You hand the car dealer $45,000 in cash. (Well, just *pretend* that you have that much cash on hand.) That's one option. Alternatively, you can pay $789 per month for six years ... and end up paying a total of $56,808. What have you done by paying the car off over time? You've paid an additional $11,808 that *could* have been spent in other ways. Wouldn't you rather have the Lexus *and* the $11,808?

Getting into debt sentences you to a lower standard of living in the future. I'm not going to tell you that you shouldn't ever have debt, but I do want you to be aware of the consequences so that you can make that decision for yourself. Personally, I'm in favor of being free of consumer debt. The interesting thing is that getting into debt isn't just an economic decision. If you think about it, it is also a psychological and spiritual decision. Let's start with the economic end first.

Are there times when it might *not* make economic sense to pay off a loan? Yes. Let's say, for example, that you have recently consolidated your consumer debt into a low-interest second mortgage or home equity line of credit (HELOC). The money paid on the loan is also tax-deductible, thus lowering your real cost of borrowing even farther. If other investment options such as stocks are earning a rate of return higher than your second mortgage or HELOC rate, you are better off putting your excess dollars into stock rather than paying off your mortgage. From a psychological and spiritual standpoint, however, the inner peace you might obtain by paying off the second mortgage or HELOC may outweigh the advantage of getting a higher return.

There are two roads here. One is the more direct road to wealth (putting the money in stocks or other investments with higher returns), and one is more scenic (the psychological freedom of having the second mortgage paid off). It's your choice. Just realize that when you do have debt, you have compounding working against you rather than for you.

Another consideration: The closer you get to being free of consumer debt, the less those out-of-the-blue, unexpected, oddball expenses will concern you. You'll have more of a "cushion" in your budget and can even start putting money into a special emergency fund.

Note: Housing debt is another topic altogether. There are some very interesting books on the pros and cons of maintaining mortgage debt. There are diverse views and it will do you good to research both sides of the question before you make your choices.

## ACTION STEPS

1. Realize that having debt sentences you to a lower standard of living in the future.

2. Understand that there are "logical" choices and "psychological and spiritual" choices. They are different roads with different outcomes, but that doesn't matter. Take the road that is "right" for you.

# Fortune Teller

## One word makes a world of difference.

Would you like to be able to predict *anyone's* financial fortune? To a very great extent, you already can! I can predict *your* financial fortune in the very same way. What is the technique? You just need to listen to the words people say about money every day. Are you using words that "speak poor?" Speak poor, and you'll be poor. On the other hand, if you learn to "speak rich," you'll start to change your entire outlook and completely transform your finances for the better.

Here is an example to help you see what I mean. If you are speaking poor, you might say, "I'm broke." Is that the message you want to send the world? Is that what you want to be true in your life? Consider these two sentences: "I'll never be rich," and "I'll always be rich." Only one word has changed, but that one word makes a world of difference. The more often we make positive statements about our finances, the more likely our finances are to improve. So why not learn to speak rich?

What might you say if you were speaking rich? Here are three examples:

- "I am going to invest and do a great job of it."
- "I have debt, and I am paying it off."
- "We will be able to afford a house soon."

If you are ever about to say, "I will never get out of debt," ask yourself, "Is this what I want to be true?" Of course it isn't, so don't say it! Rephrase what you're trying to express until it *is* something you want to be true. Every time you're about to speak about your money, ask yourself this same essential question, then speak only when the answer is yes. In this case, you might say, "Every day I am getting further out of debt."

Instead of "I'll never get out from under these lousy bills," you might say, "Slowly but surely, I am putting my finances in order."

Instead of "I'm an impulse spender—a shopaholic. I can't help it," try saying, "I spend only what I can afford to spend."

Instead of "I just can't save money," change your sentence to "I am beginning to save a little from every paycheck."

Listen to the words you use when it comes to money. If you slip and say something negative, simply take it back. Say, "I didn't mean that." Then rephrase what you've said to reflect what you want to be true.

## ACTION STEPS

1. Consciously monitor all the words you say concerning your money.
2. Use only positive statements about your money.
3. Would a farmer who wanted to harvest corn plant seeds for beans? No. Farmers plant seeds for exactly the kind of harvest they want. Do you want a fruitful money harvest? Choose to plant positive money seeds.

# Free Money

## Nothing beats the feeling of putting one over on the uncle.

How can you get free money? Well, my first thought was, "Just steal it from your employer!" Okay, yes, I hear you. You can't just go around stealing money from your company. That's not legal. Though if you are caught and go to jail, you'll at least get free room and board. But alas, you won't find the best neighbors in jail, so let's skip that plan.

Here's plan B. Imagine this situation: There is a new grocery store in a neighborhood across the country from you. To attract customers, this store agrees that for a limited time, they will match dollar for dollar all the money their customers spend in their store. All of a sudden, the customers are getting twice the amount of groceries for the same amount of money they were spending before. (Those dirty dogs! Why couldn't that store have been in *our* town?) It's like those customers are getting free money. Do you think shoppers would flock to the store? Of course they would.

Now imagine that you are offered a similar opportunity. (Yahoo! Now we're talking!) Will you take advantage of it? Your answer is likely to be "yes," but the odds say you are ignoring an opportunity right in front of you that's just as good.

What's the opportunity? It is the 401(k) plan. Does your employer offer one? Does your company offer to match dollar for dollar a certain amount or percentage of your income? If they do and you aren't taking advantage of it, you are "leaving free groceries in the store" and passing up a chance to legally take money from your employer! This is one game you *must* play if it is available to you. Put in the maximum that your company will match. Is there another place in the investment world where you can get a 100 percent match on the dollars you invest? If there is, I've never seen it.

Let's say you work for Microsoft. If you do, and they have a 401(k) plan like the one described above, guess what? You're getting some of "Uncle Bill's" money![25] Cool. He has plenty to share, so why shouldn't you have some of it? If you don't work for Microsoft but do work for another company with a 401(k) plan, just substitute your CEO's first name and get some of "Uncle Ed's" money, or "Aunt Carly's money," etc. They aren't worried; they can write it off.

---

[25] Referring, of course, to founder Bill Gates.

Wait—there's more! The dollars you contribute can be *pre-tax* dollars, meaning that every dollar you pay in is taken off your yearly income and never taxed. Yes, you'll pay tax eventually when you take the money out. And there is a 10 percent penalty tax from the IRS if you withdraw the money before age 59½. Nevertheless, the enormous up-front benefits of the tax break and employer matching make this an exceptional way to save.

Is that the end of the story? No, there is one *more* benefit I haven't mentioned yet. Uncle Sam is taxing you on your income, right? But the 401(k) money goes into the 401(k) without being taxed. So let's say you are in the 28 percent tax bracket. If you make a dollar, you take home only seventy-two cents after tax, right? The math says yes. So if you put a full dollar into the 401(k), the *real* cost to you is only seventy-two cents! Uncle Sam is subsidizing your contribution by not taxing you on each of those dollars. For every dollar you contribute, it's as if you're contributing seventy-two cents of your money and Uncle Sam is adding twenty-eight cents of his money.

That's a little tricky to understand, but here's the bottom line: When you contribute a dollar to your 401(k), your paycheck only goes down by seventy-two cents. The higher your tax bracket, the more your generous uncle contributes and the less comes out of your paycheck. Cool! Here's one time when it's *nice* to be in a higher tax bracket.

I don't know about you, but I like this plan. I like having all my money going to work for me instead of having Uncle take twenty-eight cents or more out of every dollar I make. Nothing beats the feeling of putting one over on the uncle. *So there, you slimy snake!* (Sorry, I have a hard time restraining my exuberance on this one.)

By now you should really be smiling—you can take money from your employer *and* from your not-usually-so-benevolent Uncle Sam, and you can do it all legally! What could be better than that?[26]

ACTION STEPS

1. Find out the first name of the CEO of your company (assuming you don't already know it!)

2. Put this sentence on your to-do list, filling in your CEO's first name in the blank: "Start taking some of _____'s money legally."

3. Go to your human resources department, get the forms to start or increase your 401(k), fill them out, and submit them. Make sure to include the

---

[26] Not much could be better than that. Well, okay, so there is one thing, but just one. Are you curious? Check out "That Guy's Game" later in this section.

authorization to have your monthly deduction taken directly from your checking account. If you never see the money, it's a lot harder to spend it.

4. Start smiling. Everyone will wonder what you've been up to, and what you've been up to is ...

5. ... taking your employer's money, and doing so legally!

6. ... taking Uncle Sam's money, and doing so legally!

7. Start yelling, "Hoo-hah!" and dancing around. You are getting richer and using other people's money to do it!

# Fund-a-mentals

## Failing to plan is a common reason that many people experience financial disaster.

Some people have found it useful to set up several separate money funds for different purposes. For example, one might be your emergency fund. Another might be called the "prosperity fund." This would hold dollars you are planning to invest and save long-term for retirement and old age.

One of the best funds to start is a "large expense" fund. This is an account where you can save for those larger items that come up infrequently: property taxes, home remodeling, appliance replacement, insurance renewals, Christmas gifts, and so on. Failing to plan for these larger expenses in advance is a common reason that many people experience financial disaster. Make sure you plan ahead.

You might also consider building a "fortune fund." You may be gainfully employed in an occupation that allows you to bring home a paycheck, but is it even close to your dream occupation? Why not build a fund that will eventually help you amass enough surplus to leave your current job and follow that dream you've always wanted to pursue? You may be able to earn a *living* in your current job, but why settle for that? You may earn a *fortune* if you can switch to a job that fills you with passion.

Finally, you might think about building an "annual income fund." This fund is a long-term fund for which your goal is to build enough capital to eventually return an income stream equal to your current annual income. This is an exciting fund to build; once you're finished building it, you will have officially become independently wealthy!

ACTION STEPS

1. Decide on your dreams.
2. Set up and start filling the cash accounts that will lead to your financial independence:
   - Your emergency fund: enough spare cash to cover three to six months of expenses.
   - Your prosperity fund: cash for retirement and old age.

- Your large expense fund: for those big bills that come up less frequently.
- Your fortune fund: enough money to finally pursue those lifelong dreams and let go of the job that's just paying the bills.
- Your annual income fund: enough money invested to yield an amount equal to your annual income.

# Half and Half

## Finding the fastest way to reduce your financial stress.

At the financial seminars I present, I am sometimes asked an interesting question: "If I have substantial debts and no emergency savings, which should I work on first?"

At first, my answer was purely a technical one: "First put your money toward whichever of the two has the highest interest rate. If the credit card is charging you 18 percent and you would receive only 3 from a savings account, pay off the debt first."

After a while, I decided I had a better answer—one that started with a question. "Which causes you to lose more sleep: your worries about your debt, or your worries about not having an emergency fund?" From a purely mathematical standpoint, it may be smarter to pay off the debts first, but if the lack of an emergency fund is causing you more stress, then reduce the stress first.

That's still a very good answer. Recently, however, I had a discussion with a couple who gave me another interesting idea, one that I now add to my "official" answer. The "game" we came up with is one I call "Half and Half." Having no emergency fund was actually causing this couple more stress than the significant debt they were in. "How much money would you need in an emergency fund in order to relieve that stress?" I asked.

"About $500," they answered.

Here was our solution: Set up a savings account for your emergency fund. Let it build up to, say, $1,000. Then take half of that money ($500) and apply it to your debts. Leave the other $500 in place for any emergencies and let the account build up to $1,000 again. Every time the account reaches $1,000, take another $500 and put it toward your debts. So half the $1,000 will always remain in the account as your emergency fund, and you can start paying off your debts as well.

This solution, while perhaps not the best "textbook" solution, was in reality the one that did the best job of reducing the financial stress this couple was feeling. So now my official answer includes this revised suggestion: "Whatever solution leads to the greatest peace of mind and the greatest reduction in stress is your personal best answer, no matter what the so-called experts say."

ACTION STEPS

1. Consider your debts and your need for an emergency fund. Which situation is causing you more stress?

2. Put the majority of the excess money you have from playing these games toward whichever goal will reduce your stress the fastest.

3. Remember that you don't have to put all the money toward one goal or the other. It may be that putting some money toward each of the goals will actually reduce your stress the most.

4. Make your progress visual. Charts showing your debt decreasing and your emergency fund increasing will help to reinforce the good things you are doing!

# HOK and GOK (a.k.a. "Meet Mr. Murphy")

## It may rain on your parade someday.

What is the first thing any good financial advisor will tell a new client to do? Build up an emergency fund. (Though I didn't think of this, I love the idea of calling it the "Murphy Fund" after Murphy's Law, which says, "If something can go wrong, it will.")

This is the fund you build up for those HOK or GOK items. (**H**eaven **O**nly **K**nows or **G**od **O**nly **K**nows what might befall you!) It may rain on your parade someday (unless it's the Rose Parade), and believe me, if it does, you will certainly be glad you've stashed the cash.

So how much should you set aside for emergencies? If you follow traditional thinking or the standard rule of thumb, you should set aside three to six months of living expenses as an emergency reserve. That's about $8,000 to $16,000 for the average U.S. household.

Here are some factors to consider when coming up with your own amount:

1. Your foreseeable expenses. If you know you are going to need a large amount of cash in the near future for a down payment on a house, a child's education, etc., increase your Murphy Fund to include those amounts.

2. The amount of your insurance. If you have excellent medical insurance, disability insurance, and life insurance, you can lessen the total in your Murphy Fund. If you have any concerns about whether or not you have enough insurance coverage, increase Mr. Murphy's reserves.

3. The stability of your job. If you have any doubts about the permanence of your career, increase your savings. If your job is stable, your reserve can be smaller.

4. Your number of income sources. If you or your family have only one primary income, Mr. Murphy's reserve should be increased. If you have income from multiple sources, including income from investments and inheritances, Mr. Murphy says you can decrease your total stockpile.

5. The stability of your income. If your income is commission-based, you are self-employed, or there are other factors such as seasonal fluctuations which

make your income less stable than most, Mr. Murphy says, "Save more." If your earnings are secure and increasing, Mr. Murphy says, "You rock!" Less rather than more.

## ACTION STEPS

1. Meet Mr. Murphy. Whatever can go wrong probably will. Know that in advance and plan ahead to have a financial reserve.

2. Find a thumb and follow its rule.

3. Make a list of the above five factors to consider and put pluses or minuses next to each depending on whether your evaluations indicate you should save more or less. Adjust your final Murphy Fund total accordingly.

4. Rest well. The greater the Murphy Fund you have in place, the more peaceful your siesta will be.

# Just Desserts

## Dramatically reduce your restaurant bills while still having fun.

Who's the best cook in your house? (Fill in your name or your significant other's or roommate's name here.) Is it Bob or Carol, Ted or Alice, Jim or Frank, Julie or Debbie? Maybe you are both equally qualified. It doesn't matter. Determine a "cook of the week," and you can find some ways to dramatically reduce your restaurant bills while still having fun. Have you been nominated to be "cook" this week? If so, read on. You may get to *like* being the cook!

If you would normally go out for a nice, five-course dinner with appetizers, drinks, and dessert, consider this: Why not have wine and appetizers at home? You can get them inexpensively. Discount stores like Costco have great prices on wine and many "heat and serve" appetizers, if you want to minimize the cooking. Add an inexpensive wine,[27] and your "cooking" is done! How can that be? It's because you can then leave the house, head for a local restaurant, and let someone else cook the rest of your meal. (All of a sudden this "cook" job is sounding a lot better, isn't it?)

It will amaze you how much you can reduce your restaurant bills by having your alcohol at home. If you also have your appetizers at home, they will reduce your hunger before you head to the restaurant, thereby helping you eat and spend less. You have two home runs already, and you've barely warmed up the oven.

Now, once you arrive at your favorite dining establishment, why not split an entrée? This is easy in the many restaurants that have large portions. If you can't agree on an entrée, just eat half of your meal, and you'll each have a second meal to eat later. Alternatively, you can have your romantic dinner at home (Bob or Carol's restaurant), then go out for your favorite dessert and after-dinner coffee. (Oh look, it's the title of this game: "Just Desserts!")

Finally, watch for specials at your restaurants. You can often save money simply by eating out during the week or earlier in the evening. The "cook" makes

---

[27] In California, we have a great selection of inexpensive wines from a variety of places. One in particular, Charles Shaw ("Two-buck Chuck") actually makes a couple of surprisingly drinkable wines at $1.99 per bottle. Not that I've tried them, of course.

the decisions and has the final word on which courses should be consumed at home.

See? I told you "cook" was a great job!

*Bon appetite!*

## ACTION STEP

1. Look for ways to creatively reduce the amount of money you spend eating out at restaurants.

# Machine Gun

## If your finances are wounded and
## your debt is killing you, start here first.

Okay, you've come to this game because you need some serious firepower. You need a *lot* of money-saving ideas, and you need them fast! Your finances are wounded, and your debt is killing you. You need to fight back fast and fight back hard.

Some of these ideas are expanded in other games, but you get the quick and dirty versions here. Here you go: A long list of money-saving ideas. You can skim them quickly, gather the "bullets" that you like, and start shooting.

- Defer a car purchase for another year; buying used is usually a better deal. If you buy new, try to do it near the end of the month and/or end of the model year. Most companies have sales quotas to meet, and month end is a good time to get a car at a lower price.
- Buy one new suit this year instead of two.
- Refinance your mortgage.
- Plan vacations far enough in advance to get super-saver airline tickets.
- Vacation during the off-season, when rates are lower.
- Avoid ATMs that charge fees.
- Use electronic banking. Many online banks will actually send a paper check through the mail to any person or vendor that doesn't accept electronic transfers. Mine even pays the postage for me!
- Clip grocery coupons from the newspaper.
- Caulk and weather-strip doors and windows that need it.
- Keep the thermostat a little lower in winter and higher in summer.
- If you need to leave certain lights, like your kid's bathroom lights, switched on through the night, install some of the new, energy-efficient bulbs. They use less power and last up to ten times longer.
- Let dishes air dry in the dishwasher.
- Use a clothesline when the weather's right.

- Cut down on fast food and eating out.
- Drink water instead of coffee, tea, or soda.
- Rent more DVDs instead of seeing movies at the theater.
- Go to the cheaper matinee shows at the theater rather than paying full price.
- Brown-bag it one or two days a week instead of eating your lunches at restaurants.
- Change your own oil.
- Clean your own carpet.
- Grow your own vegetables or fruits.
- Wash your own car.
- Mow your own lawn.
- Clean your own house or lessen the frequency of outside cleaning help.
- Cook your own meals.
- Do your own laundry.
- Decrease or eliminate your consumption of premium drinks like Starbucks.
- Buy plain old sunglasses instead of designer eyewear; the same goes for underwear.
- Buy used exercise and sporting equipment.
- Step one notch down from buying state-of-the-art electronics; get the "just prior" version and save big!
- Have a garage sale if you have a larger number of TVs, VCRs, DVD players, iPods, etc. than the number of people in your family.
- Use disposable razors.
- Ditch the expensive juice boxes for the kids.
- Drink regular beer instead of premium brands.
- Stop buying lottery tickets.
- Buy drugstore brand cosmetics instead of department store brands.
- Buy one pair of shoes instead of two or more pairs.
- Refill bottled water bottles from the sink rather than tossing them and buying new ones.
- Cancel seldom-used health club memberships.

- Just say no to elective cosmetic surgery and dentistry.

- Lose the personal trainer and the massages.

- Drop extra phone features like call waiting, call forwarding, and caller ID.

- Consume "ordinary" brand ice creams and cookies instead of premium brands.

- Stop buying hardcover books you'll only read once. Get them from your library! (Ours rents current bestsellers for $1 per week.)

- Wear your old sweats instead of buying fancy, new exercise clothes.

- Vacation locally or stay with and mooch off relatives. (They deserve some payback, right?)

- Press clothes at home instead of using the dry cleaners.

- Skip one week per month of the things you tend to do weekly, such as frequenting restaurants and/or movie theaters.

- Take the free cell phone that comes with your service rather than buying the $250 Corvette model.

- Cut flowers from a garden you plant rather than buying fresh flowers every week.

## ACTION STEPS

1. Pick your bullets and load the gun. (Decide on at least three actions you can take from the above list.)

2. Aim. (Set some dollar goals you want to reach as a result of taking action.)

3. Optional: Yell "Duck!" before pulling the trigger. (Exception: If your name is Dick and you work with a president, you are exempt.)

4. Start shooting.

# Mostly Old Numbers

## If you spend the money now, it's gone.

Have you ever gotten a raise or a bonus? Have you ever received some unexpected cash? Have you received an inheritance? What did you do with the extra income? Do you even know? If I asked you to, could you look back and tell me exactly what you did with your newfound wealth? If you are like most people, the answer would be no. Why is that? There could be many reasons, but the bottom line is usually that we are not making conscious decisions related to money and are choosing by default to increase our standards of living.

"But I worked hard for that raise," you might be saying. "I deserve to spend the extra money." I certainly won't argue that with you; I work hard too, and it is definitely nice to feel like you have been rewarded for all your efforts. My point has to do with the default choice you made rather than the conscious choice you could have made. The default choice (spend now) is always a short-term choice. If you spend the money now, it is gone. But if you make a conscious choice to save and invest just a *portion* of the money, you can enjoy returns on your hard work for the rest of your life!

"Old Numbers" is an easy game you can learn in about two minutes but that will have you richer before a year is out. Here's how to play: Whenever you get a raise, choose to keep living on your old salary. Then take your salary increase and put that amount toward increasing your savings and investing. You can even set up a preauthorized withdrawal that goes into an investment of your choice before you even get your paycheck. Then, when you do get those checks, all seems just as it was before. Instead of changing your spending habits because of your additional income, you continue getting the same size paycheck and spending just as you were before.

This same concept works well for money you receive from unexpected sources. If someone repays you a loan you'd forgotten about, if an inheritance comes in, or if a business expense reimbursement that you had forgotten about comes back, just invest the newfound wealth and continue right on living by the "Old Numbers."

"But then I don't feel rewarded for all my hard work!" I can hear you saying. Don't worry. If that's the case, just read on to the next game …

ACTION STEPS

1. Plan ahead for your next raise. (Plan, that is, to continue living as if you hadn't gotten the raise.)[28]

2. Watch for that unexpected, extra cash that shows up now and then. When it comes, just invest the newfound wealth and continue your normal lifestyle.

3. There is no number three. I just wanted to see if you were actually paying attention here.

4. Skip step three since there wasn't one.

5. Plant those monetary seeds and watch them grow! Remember: The more seeds you plant, the bigger your harvest will be!

---

[28] Unless, of course, you are presently living beyond your means. If so, just forget this game. There are *other* games you'd better try first!

# New Numbers

**The game for anyone who's ever said "God, give me patience ... and give it to me *now*, please!"**

Are you feeling bummed out because "Old Numbers" didn't let you spend any of that additional money you worked so hard to earn? Well, don't forget that even though you aren't spending the seeds (dollars) you are planting, you will eventually get to spend the crop (interest) they produce. If you can be patient, you will eventually have *larger* amounts of money to spend than if you had spent them up front. Of course, that's not always easy in our "God, give me patience, and give it to me *now*, please" society.

I will concede that "Old Numbers" doesn't give you the immediate gratification that spending now does. Therefore, as an alternative, you could consider the game I call "New Numbers." You might call it "Halfway House," because what you'll do is invest half of your new raise or unexpected income and spend the other half. Then you'll feel happy in *two* ways! You'll be happy spending part of the money, but you'll also be happy that your future fortune is growing as well.

The bottom line: You can spend, save, or invest your newfound money in any proportions you wish. Just make conscious decisions about your money and consider the ultimate rewards you'll enjoy as a result of saving even a portion of it for later.

ACTION STEPS

1. Play "Old Numbers" (the previous game).

2. Get bummed because you can't spend anything extra.

3. Ignore my prior advice, plant (save) a few less seeds, and eat (spend) some of your crop now! Isn't it fun being rebellious?

4. If you save half of your new income, then you can still eat, drink, and be Mary[29] with the other half. Just be conscious about it. For every dollar you save now, you'll be able to spend more dollars later.

---

[29] That would be Mary as in "Mary, Mary, quite contrary." Note: If you are male and you want to be Mary, you'll have to wait for Halloween.

# Pajama Party

## Put your passbook in pj's, but never let it sleep at home.

Have you ever been to a pajama party? Everybody comes to the party in their jammies. While you're there, everyone eats, drinks, plays games, stays awake as late as possible, spends the night, and then goes home the next day. At least that's how I remember them.

In this game, we want your money to have the pajama party, and the party will be held at the *post office*. (No, we won't be going into *that* game! In this case, we mean the real post office.)

"Why would I want my money to spend the night at the post office?" you might wisely be asking. The answer is this: Because it will be on its way to your bank, where its job will be to rapidly accumulate interest for you until you have enough money to invest part of it elsewhere!

"Okay, that all sounds fine and dandy," I can hear you saying, "but I still don't get it. What exactly am I supposed to be doing here?"

Oh, you ask such great questions! Here's your answer:

Open a passbook savings account at your bank. I'm assuming you already have a checking account, but if not, you'll need to open one of those as well. Take the passbook home and immediately write a check (a small amount, even a dollar, will do just fine) to be deposited in that account. Take the passbook and the check and send them together in an envelope to the pajama party at the post office. (In other words, mail them to the bank. The post office will see to it that they attend the pajama party overnight.)

Remember that your passbook is a party animal. It *always* wants to be at that ongoing pajama party at the post office. Therefore, the rule is that the passbook can never sleep at your house. Every time your passbook comes back to you in the mail, you must write another check for a deposit (remember, a small amount is fine) and send the passbook back to the post office (on its way to the bank) that very same day.

The amounts of the deposits don't matter. What matters is the idea you are implanting in your mind—that your savings are constantly growing. If you plant a single seed one day and never water or fertilize it, what are the odds you'll ever have a thriving garden? Slim to none. However, if you plant seeds all the time and

149

are always watering and fertilizing them, you'll have a better chance at having a thriving garden.

Let that passbook party! One day you'll be rich enough to start having pajama parties every night yourself! Call me. I'll have my pj's ready.

## ACTION STEPS

1. Open a passbook savings account at your bank.
2. Immediately go home and write a check to yourself (even a small amount is okay) and send it with the passbook to the bank.
3. Each time the passbook arrives back in your mailbox, immediately write out another check to yourself and send it back to the bank that same day.
4. Never let the passbook stay in your house overnight.
5. Get out your pj's and start the party; your savings will start growing rapidly, and you'll be excited.

# Pajama Party, Version II

## It's all about learning how to have happy money.

What do you do when you get a bill in the mail? (After the weeping, sobbing, moaning, griping, cursing, stomping, and jumping up and down, that is.) When you get a bill, you *pay* it, of course. You write a check for the proper amount, and you send it off to the dastardly company that sent you the bill.

So let's go back to why aren't you saving any money. Perhaps it is because no one has ever sent you a "bill" asking you to!

Here's a fun idea I heard about recently. A young man made up some "bills" to himself that looked like they were from his bank. He decided on a monthly amount he wanted to save and made out the bills for that amount. Then he put the bills in self-addressed envelopes, gave twelve of them to a friend, and asked the friend to mail him one of the envelopes each month. When he received each "bill" from the "bank," he promptly got out his checkbook and wrote a check to "pay" the bank the amount he "owed."

In the years that followed, he continued the habit, slowly increasing the amount he "owed the bank" each month. How do you think he's done in terms of saving money over the years? If you answered "very well," you're right!

Isn't that a clever idea? Better yet, the bill payments will get to go to the pajama party at the post office along with your passbook. You'll have some of the happiest money you can imagine.

ACTION STEPS

1. Decide how much you want to save each month.

2. Make up twelve "bills" due and payable to yourself for that amount.

3. Give the twelve bills to a diligent friend or neighbor and have them mail you one of them each month.

4. Every time you receive a bill, immediately write out a check to yourself for that amount and deposit it in your savings account.

5. Slowly start increasing the amounts you "bill" yourself each month. As soon as you get comfortable with an amount, increase it just a little.

6. When people ask why you are smiling so much, tell them about this great book you read that taught you how to have happy money!

# Pennies from Heaven

## But what if the penny is upside down?

Have you ever spotted a lonely penny lying by itself on the ground? Did you bother to pick it up? Most people will just pass a penny right by, believing that such a small amount just isn't worth the effort. I have a different philosophy. No amount is too small to ignore, and no amount is too small to add to your "fortune." Have I lost my mind? Some people think so, but to you I say, "No, not at all."

Think of this: If you were to find just one penny every day of your life, and you lived for eighty years, how much money do you think you would accumulate? Are you ready for this? You would accumulate a massive $292.00. Oh, sure, you're rich now.

Amassing $292.00—that's surely not worth it, right? I beg to differ! You see, we haven't considered how much that money could grow if you invested it as you went along. Until now, we've just put our pennies in a big, fat piggy bank and left them alone for eighty years. But imagine if you were investing those pennies. At 9 percent, $3.65 per year for eighty years accumulates to almost $40,000! Hmm ... now those pennies are sounding more interesting, aren't they?

The larger point is that you need to learn to be a good steward with even small amounts. If you prove to be a worthy money manager when the amounts are small, larger amounts will come your way.

The biblical parable of the talents makes this point. In Matthew 25:21, it says: "His master praised him for good work. 'You have been faithful in handling this small amount,' he told him, 'so now I will give you many more responsibilities.'"

"But what if the penny is upside down and facing tails up?" you ask. "Isn't it bad luck to pick up a penny that's upside down?" My belief is that you make your own luck. But if it bothers you to pick up an upside-down penny, reach down and flip over the penny while it's still on the ground. Stand back up, look away, and then look back down at the ground. Well, look at that—there's a right-side-up penny! Now you can bend down and pick it up. You've just made your own luck.

Pennies are from heaven. You never know where you'll find them. You might find them on sidewalks, in parking lots, in the street, in the grocery store, in Taco Bell, you name it. Will you literally find one every day? No, but you absolutely will *average* at least one a day. Some days you'll find nickels, dimes, or quarters, and sometimes you'll even find whole handfuls of change. Once I even found $60! (That's more than sixteen *years* worth of pennies!)

Keep your eyes open, and never pass up any opportunity to add to your wealth, no matter how small. If you honor your money in small amounts, it will honor you and grow.

## ACTION STEPS

1. Find a copy of that song with the lyrics "lonely days and lonely nights." Play it over and over until you just can't get the lyrics out of your head.

2. Look for stray pennies (and their brother and sister coins), and when you see one lying by itself on the ground, hear those "lonely days and lonely nights" lyrics run through your head.

3. You can't just leave that poor, helpless penny lying there alone, now, can you? (I don't know you personally, but I'm sure you aren't that heartless.)

4. Pick up the penny (turning it right side up first if necessary), and give thanks that your wealth is increasing every day, no matter from what source.

5. Learn to honor money in every amount, whether it's small or large. As you honor money, it will honor you by growing!

# Piece of Mine

**Sharing is a wonderful privilege, not a duty.**
**Just don't give the house away.**

Yes, you read that title correctly: "Piece of Mine," not "Peace of Mind." Although in this game, the former will actually quite often lead to the latter, as you'll soon see.

If you are reading this in the United States or in any of the other wealthiest nations in the world, I can safely make this prediction about you: you have more "stuff" than you need. If you live in the United States, you are living in one of the wealthiest civilizations of all time. Many of our "middle-class" citizens live in comparative splendor and ease unknown to even the royal classes of a few hundred years ago.

Lest you doubt your place in the wealth hierarchy of this planet, let me share something that struck me with enormous impact. If you have:

- a roof over your head (either rented or owned);

- enough food to eat;

- two automobiles (one of which doesn't even have to run!);

- a hobby for which you own specialized equipment (skis, a camera, golf clubs, etc.), then …

… you are automatically in the top 5 percent of people on this planet in terms of wealth. Did that sink in? If you meet those criteria, *you are in the top 5 percent on this planet!*

Ninety of the remaining 95 percent of the world's citizens would probably trade places with you in a heartbeat, including taking on all your "troubles," in order to have the level of wealth you have obtained and the opportunities available to you.

What happened to the other 5 percent of people? They have reached a level of spiritual enlightenment in which wealth is recognized for what it is—temporary, fleeting, and soon to be gone. You can't take it with you when you leave this earthly existence. To this five percent, wealth just doesn't matter. (That, however, is the subject of a different book.)[30]

The point is merely that you have more possessions than you even use. There are items in the closets, garages, attics, and basements of nearly all of our homes that haven't been used in more than a year and will likely never be used again. So pass them on! Even in our exceptionally wealthy countries, there are many people who do not share in the abundance. For those of us who do, there is a responsibility to share. If someone else doesn't have enough, I'm usually more than glad to give him or her "a piece of mine." I say "usually" because like you, I still have much more than I need, and I must continually remind myself to weed out, to pass on, and to share.

Sharing is a wonderful privilege, not a duty. In addition to multiplying your own financial blessings, you will find that you'll be blessed with great joy and a certain peace of mind as you happily give away more of the things you consider to be a "piece of mine." Try it and see.

Let me leave you with this final thought. If you are presently in poor financial straits for whatever reason and money just doesn't seem to be flowing your way, do the most counterintuitive thing imaginable. Find someone even worse off than you are, and *give* him or her something. Don't be irresponsible, but try giving until it hurts. Keep giving until you truly can say to yourself, "I must have lost my mind to be doing this."

What will happen with your own finances at that point will be nothing short of miraculous. You will have to take what I'm telling you on faith. But try it on a small scale first—I don't want your lawyer calling me because you gave your house away!

Those of you willing to share even when you are lacking yourself will be the ones writing me letters and sending me e-mails saying, "You just won't believe what happened to me." I can't wait for those letters.

ACTION STEPS

1. Read books about how the kings and queens lived back in the eighteenth century or earlier.

2. Realize that compared to those mighty, majestic, royal relics, you are living in comparative splendor and ease. (Cool, huh?)

---

[30] Keep an eye out. That's a pretty catchy title: *The Other Five Percent.* I might just have to write that book.

3. Look around you and realize that you have more "stuff" and "junk" and "things" than you could ever possibly use. You certainly don't need fifteen sets of whozewhatzits. Fourteen sets are surely enough.

4. Weed it out, pass it on. Share.

# Pine Mountain Ragtime

## Can you spell "VROOOM?"

Recently I came across an expensive, macho-guy item that every man described as a real "chick magnet." Sweetness reigns! Yes, I'm married, but I've been overdue for my midlife crisis, and I thought, "Well, hey, I can afford the payments if this baby's a chick magnet." (Yes, that is an all-too-typical male response. Guilty as charged.)

My wife, on the other hand, was more pragmatic. Her first thought (and this will surprise you) wasn't that I shouldn't get the "boy-toy." Instead, it was that I might attract more people into our business if I *did!* (I don't think she's too worried about the chick magnet part at my age.) "Think about the people you'd meet," she said. "Men your age quite often have plenty of disposable income and have toys like that if they've been successful. What a great way to network!" she said. Okay, *that* didn't help.

Was I tempted to buy that "chick magnet?" You bet. Might I still one day take the leap and make the purchase? Yes, but not right now. You see, I'm playing a game called "Pine Mountain Ragtime." On Pine Mountain, you are allowed to "pine away" for anything your heart desires. Your imagination can run wild. No matter what the cost, you can dream about having it. You want a yacht, a mansion, a Ferrari? Pine away all you want. However, pining is all you are allowed to do—at least initially. That's step one.

Step two: Calculate how many hours it would take to earn that item you are pining for so much. In my case (okay, I'll spill the beans), that *very* high-end American Ironhorse custom chopper (i.e. motorcycle) would take about a year and a half to earn—somewhere around three thousand hours of work. Whew!

Step three: Ask yourself if it's worth that many hours of hard work to have that high-end item. For me, the answer was, "Not this week. Probably not next week either."

Step four: Remember that it's "ragtime." I'm choosing to stay in "rags" rather than silk or satin in order to stay on track for my wife's and my joint financial goals. Some of those goals, like owning a condominium in San Francisco, have more draw for me (and potential for capital gain) than that chopper that will depreciate the minute it leaves the showroom.

Is your item not quite so easy to give up? If you've calculated how many hours it will take to earn the money to pay for the item, including any finance charges, and you still want it, put a picture of it on your refrigerator for thirty days. At the end of the thirty days, ask yourself if you still really want it that badly. My refrigerator has never failed me yet. Thirty days is a long time to rethink a major expenditure, and so far, that length of time has always been enough for me to come to my senses and realize that my plans for building wealth and reducing debt are still higher priorities.

There is that thing about attracting more clients, though … I wonder if she really meant it. (As I write this, there are still twenty-one days left for that chick magnet to hang on the refrigerator.) Will I make a good decision and pass it up? Send a note to me (questions@wordsofabundance.com), and I'll let you know. Odds are that my answer will be yes.[31]

Meanwhile, if my wife wins the lotto and wants to buy it *for* me, would that be okay? Can you spell *"vrooom?"* I have to admit, though—they may ask me to stay out of the showroom. Every time they fire up that humongous engine, I leave drool on their floor. That chopper has a custom purple paint job, too. I feel magnetic already.

Pine, pine, pine.

PS: Five-carat diamonds do it for my wife, lest you think the pining is all mine.

PPS: I read recently that 86 percent of Americans felt happier after having voluntarily cut back on consumption. You'll be happier when you join them. You can thank me later.

## ACTION STEPS

1. Find a blank piece of paper and draw four vertical columns on it. Label the columns "Item," "Cost," "Hours to Earn," and "Worth It?"

2. In the first column, make a list of everything you are currently pining for. (Okay, so you may need a bunch of sheets.)

3. In the second column, write down the cost of each item, including shipping, handling, assembly if required, taxes, duty fees, maintenance costs, upkeep costs, storage costs, and every other conceivable cost of ownership.

4. Figure out your hourly salary if you don't know it already.

---

[31] You are welcome to send me any other questions you may have as a result of reading the book as well! (If you'd like *more* great ideas each month, you can also sign up for my free newsletter at www.wordsofabundance.com.)

5. Divide the number in the second column by your hourly salary and enter the result in column three. This number is the total number of hours you will need to spend working in order to obtain the item you desire.

6. Look realistically at the number of hours it will take you to earn the item and answer the question in column four: would it really be worth it?

7. Remember that if your answer in column four is no, you are not making a permanent decision not to purchase the item. You are just making that decision for now. You can make a new list any time you want and go through the process again.

8. Meanwhile, think about those 86 percent of Americans who are happier because they cut back on consumption. Once we add you to the list, we'll be at 87 percent!

# Piranha

## "Do you really want to put your hand in there?"

Remember the book titled *Swim with the Sharks without Being Eaten Alive?* Just as there are sharks in the business world, there are piranhas in the financial world. One could argue that there are actually many varieties of piranha out there, but we're going to focus on just one: the credit card companies. Now, there are many excellent credit card companies out there, don't get me wrong. However, you need to realize that they are in *business,* and companies who are in business have a goal of making what? *Profit,* that's what.

Your mission, should you choose to accept it, is to personally contribute less profit to the credit card companies and more profit to your own investments. Would you like a fun mental game to help you make that happen? Try this one. I call it "Piranha."

Imagine that piranhas have miraculously become our new legal tender. As a result, your wallet or purse is filled with swarming, vicious piranhas. Every time you are tempted to make a purchase and reach in your wallet or purse for some legal tender, imagine your hand being attacked by those voraciously hungry fish with viciously sharp teeth. Do you really want to put your hand in there?

Piranhas (cunningly disguised as your credit cards) are not your friends. Every night, they eat up all the cash in your savings account, your checkbook, and your wallet. Even worse, come the next morning, they are still hungry and looking for more of your hard-earned cash to consume.

Odds are good that you have credit card debt. Most consumers do. That debt costs you interest, maybe even exorbitant interest. Every dollar of interest you have to pay is a dollar that is no longer available for building your fortune. Is that really what you want? If not, then the next time you're about to use that credit card, ask yourself whose fortune you really want to build—your own, or the credit card company's. I hope that you already realized the dangers of credit card debt before I mentioned it. Have you started working on paying off your credit card debt? If so, good for you! If not, why not start now? Climb out of your hole.

Here's some great advice for anyone who has dug himself or herself into a hole: *stop digging!* It is great that you are working on paying off your credit card debt, but how efficient is it to fill in a hole by shoveling in two shovelfuls of dirt and then shoveling one back out? That's what happens when you continue using your cards while trying to pay them off!

Do you need some quick ideas to help you stop using your credit cards? Here are some possibilities. You can decide which one(s) might work for you.

- Destroy the credit cards entirely and close the accounts.
- Keep only *one* credit card, put that one in an empty soup can filled with water, and freeze it. (Why the soup can? It's metal. You won't be able to use the microwave oven to get the card out!)
- Use a "no balance allowed" credit card.
- Use a debit card instead of a credit card.
- Use only cash.

If you keep a credit card, just remember those sharp teeth and those voracious appetites whenever you are tempted to open your wallet and pull it out. Even one piranha can leave your fingers (and finances) sore and bleeding. Is it worth it?

Okay, so visualizing piranhas in your wallet is unusual, to say the least. Nevertheless, if a crazy visual image helps you make a better decision, who's to say it's so crazy?

## ACTION STEPS

1. Remember that banks are in business to make a profit, not to be your best friends.

2. Imagine that the credit cards in your wallet are piranhas.

3. Carry some spare Band-Aids at all times. Until you toughen up, your fingers may be a little bloody.

4. Optional: Put some ketchup on your fingers and cover them with Band-Aids. When asked about what happened to your fingers, tell everyone about the piranha in your wallet. (You may get a free white coat with weird sleeves, a room of your own, and some heavy medications for a while, but you'll have a fun story for your grandkids someday.)

# Recliner

## Is eighteen years long enough?

Do you have long-term goals for reducing debt or accumulating savings? If you have a specific goal for either or both that is at least one year away, try this game.

First, start keeping a chart or graph of your goal(s) and your progress toward meeting them. Perhaps you have a goal to pay off a certain credit card in the next twelve months. Or maybe you've paid off the credit cards already and want to build an emergency fund of a certain size this year.

To speed up the progress toward your goal, any time you "need" something or other, ask yourself if it could wait a year. Maybe you have (as we do) an old recliner. Ours is at least eighteen years old and sorely in need of replacing. Can we wait one more year to replace it and apply the money we're saving now toward meeting our one-year financial goals? Yes, of course.

We also have a washer and dryer that are just hanging onto life out of sheer stubbornness. Our best guess is that they may be around sixteen years old. We even have the money set aside to purchase new ones once these officially go to appliance heaven, but in the meantime, we've already held onto them twenty-four months longer than we'd originally intended. The money for the new appliances is earning interest for us in the meantime. Would it be nice to have a new washer and dryer? You better believe it. But we decided that we would rather wait and use the temporary savings to help meet our current-year goals.

Is your electric can opener broken? Could you use your old-fashioned, hand-operated opener for a year and then replace the electric one? Yes. It might not be quite as convenient, but you need to have a manual opener anyway just in case the electricity goes out and you need to open the cat food.

ACTION STEPS

1. Set your financial goals and start tracking your progress while sitting in a very old recliner.

2. Be sure you have a manual can opener in the house (and know how to use it!)

3. Have your washer and dryer call my washer and dryer. Old folks enjoy sharing "war stories" with each other.

4. Whenever you want to replace something in your home, see if you can wait a full year before you replace the item. Wait two years if the old item is your spouse.

5. Start telling everyone that you've started a new hobby—collecting antiques![32]

6. Let the money you are saving earn interest for that extra year, and put the interest you earn into your investments.

---

[32] Wisdom from the war zone: Never refer to your spouse as one of the antiques.

# "That Guy's" Game

## A game so good you'll need to be wary.

You know the guy—that one named Roth. He has this game where you pay taxes on your income up front and then set aside up to $5,000—or more, depending on the tax year and your age—of after-tax dollars each year for your future retirement (in a Roth IRA).

So what's so great about that? Two things:

1.  All the money builds tax-free from year to year.

2.  If you wait at least five years for it to grow and then 59½ to withdraw the funds, you'll get to withdraw *all* the funds (your initial dollars *and* the gain) tax-free!

I won't go into all the tax rules here, as they change from year to year. Please consult your tax advisor. Not everyone is eligible for a Roth IRA, but if you are, jump all over this one, and jump fast. This may be the most incredible giveaway that the government allows in our lifetimes. In fact, it is *so* good that you need to be very wary of … (see the title of the next game!)

ACTION STEPS

1.  Whenever you are dealing with the government, be sure you are watching out for "that guy." (If he has a badge, do whatever he asks.)

2.  Check with your tax advisor and find out if you qualify for a Roth IRA.

3.  If you do, put as much as you legally can into it as soon as possible.

4.  Keep putting money into it for as many years as it is available and you qualify.

5.  Leave the money invested until you are at least 59½, then start taking it out tax-free!

6.  Send me 1 percent of your withdrawals as a "Thanks for the advice!" remuneration. That's a small amount. You'll never miss it.

# Uncle Wiggly

## Don't leave your money on this uncle's table.

Have you ever noticed how often the U.S. government changes its mind? Taxes go up. Taxes go down. Laws are approved. Laws are struck down. Two-dollar bills appear; two-dollar bills disappear. Nothing ever seems to stay put permanently.

Let this be a lesson to you. Uncle Sam (in this case, I'll call him Uncle Wiggly) is known for changing the rules just when you finally figure out the game. So to play and win against your uncle, you must know the rules (or hire someone who does), then take advantage of any time that the rules are in your favor.

You'll notice I mention our wiggly uncle right after mentioning that guy Roth. Are you wondering why? It is because the government stands to lose huge amounts of future tax dollars by letting us have Roth IRAs. Our Roth IRAs will eventually pay out millions of dollars worth of growth, and our uncle can't collect taxes on that money! Do you think he'll figure that out one of these days? I do. So if you have a chance to benefit even temporarily from a tax law like the one that established the Roth IRA, do so immediately and without hesitation. You can bet that if it sounds too good to be true, your uncle will eventually wiggle his way out of it.

Know the laws, and take advantage of every legal deduction for which you can qualify. Don't let a lack of knowledge on your part leave even a dollar of your money sitting on Uncle Wiggly's table. Will Uncle be good-natured and jolly and give it back to you since you shouldn't have left it there? Personally, I wouldn't count on it. Uncle Wiggly's record speaks otherwise.

Get professional advice if you need to. The cost of the advice may be small in proportion to your potential gains.

ACTION STEPS

1.  Know the tax laws or hire someone who does.

2.  Take advantage of every available legitimate tax break you can get.

3.  If a law is favorable to you now, take advantage of it to the maximum extent that Uncle Wiggly allows.

4.  Plan as if the laws will eventually change, because they will.

# What's in Your Pocket(book)?

## The one game neurotics always win.

How do you arrange the money in your purse or wallet? Is it neat and tidy, all facing the same direction, and ordered by denomination? Or is it rumpled, turned every which way, stuffed in willy-nilly, and disorganized? Maybe your money isn't even in your wallet at all. Maybe it's just crammed into a purse or pocket in a wadded-up mess.

According to my own informal, unscientific survey, it appears that there is a correlation between how neat and tidy people keep their money and how well their financial lives are progressing. My theory is that the neat and tidy folks generally have more successful financial lives than those in the disorganized, rumpled, or crammed-in categories.

Is there a good, scientific reason why that should be so? No. Could there be a spiritual component in the sense that those who "honor" money by keeping it organized attract more money into their lives? My suspicion is that there could be.

Pretend this game is called "Rabbit" and that you are being asked to perform the following imaginary experiment. Find someone who owns a large farm. Ask the farmer if he/she will let you board two separate groups of rabbits on the farm—one group at each end, completely separate from each other.

When the farm owner says yes, put the two groups of bunnies in place. From day one, do everything possible to be certain that one group of bunnies is pampered, spoiled, and lacks nothing that would make them happy. Their home should be clean and tidy with pillow-top mattresses and caviar for all. (Or else feed them whatever tastes to them like Hostess Twinkies do to me, a food substance that must certainly be similar to manna from heaven. What might that be for rabbits? Truthfully, I've never asked them.)

For group two, think of every way you could possibly irritate them and keep them constantly agitated and on edge. Make sure their home is a mess, that they have saggy, uncomfortable mattresses to sleep on, and that their food is always cold. (Unless, of course the food is *supposed* to be cold, in which case you should make it warm.)

Which group of rabbits do you think would multiply the fastest? Did I hear you say "The ones that are treated well?" Hmm. What if your money responded in the same way? Would you think about changing how you treat it?

If you are in the "untidy" category I described above, try this for one month. Keep all your money neatly ordered by denomination and facing the same direction. See what happens, and let me know. I'll bet my neat and tidy money that as you start treating your money with honor and respect, your financial life will improve.

Try it and let me know.

## ACTION STEPS

1. Take all the money out of your wallet.

2. Send it to me. (Please note that step two is optional.)

3. Arrange all the money in order by denomination (first the Catholic money, then the Baptist, then the Methodist, etc.)

4. Place all the money back into your wallet in an exceptionally orderly and tidy way.

5. Repeat these steps at least once per day—or better yet, every time you open your wallet.

6. Give this idea a fair test of at least thirty days. It will improve your financial life!

# Wheels of Fortune

## Driving like a millionaire.

If you are truly serious about getting rich, I'd like to recommend a very enlightening book to you. It's called *The Millionaire Next Door,* by Thomas J. Stanley. It is a fascinating study of people who are millionaires and what they have in common. Wouldn't it be interesting to know how they make purchases, what kinds of lifestyles they live (not what you'd expect!), and how they got to be millionaires in the first place? *The Millionaire Next Door* has those answers!

I first read the book while I was still on my way to hitting that magic, million-dollar net worth mark, and what I learned from it not only helped me gain my first million, it is *still* helping me toward earning additional millions. If someone has accumulated a million dollars or more and that happens to be your goal as well, wouldn't it be worth spending some money on a book that tells you how they did it? Of course it would. That's why you bought *this* book, right?

Some of the most interesting (and surprising) information that I learned from *The Millionaire Next Door* was in the section on the types of cars that millionaires drive. I expected Mercedes, Jaguars, Rolls-Royces, Ferraris, and other exotics. Was I right? No. The most common brand of car owned by millionaires, as related by the book, is Ford. (Okay, that's amazing!) And the most common Ford owned by millionaires at the time of the book's publication was the Ford Explorer.[33] Do you want to know what is even more amazing? The millionaires typically *didn't* buy them new.

Hearing about the Ford Explorer was tremendously exciting to me, because I happened to own a Ford Explorer at the time I read the book. I will admit to buying a Mercedes sometime later, but I kept the Mercedes for seven years and then sold it to buy another Explorer. If those Fords are good enough for other millionaires, they're surely good enough for me.

As I mentioned in the footnote, it may well be that the Explorer isn't the most common vehicle today, what with our astronomical gasoline prices. Moreover, if you are a Chevy or GM person, cool beans. Toyota, Hyundai, and other brands

---

[33] Remember, the book *The Millionaire Next Door* was written a few years ago, before today's high fuel prices. I'd be curious to see the results if that same study were done today. Maybe now it would be the Hybrid Ford Escape or something more fuel-efficient. If you do a study, let me know.

are acceptable too. The point is that good value, excellent reliability, and economy still dictate what vehicles most millionaires buy.

To go back to an earlier point that I didn't expand on, recall that the Explorers in question were often purchased used. Why lose so much money in depreciation by buying a new car? Let other people take the hit on the initial depreciation and then pick up a great value a couple years later when they get tired of the car. You can get some great deals on used cars with low mileage that are in great shape and have many miles left in them. We purchased one of our vehicles when it was two years old, and it only had 15,000 miles on it. It was in great shape, and we procured it for nearly half the original cost. Wow! Better yet, it gets better gas mileage than the Explorer we still have. Guess which one gets the most use? (Hint: It's not the Explorer.)

Are you curious if there might in fact *be* a millionaire living next door to you? Do your neighbors have a Ford Explorer or other long-held, economical vehicle that they use every day? The money they are saving may well be the same money that has pushed their net worth past the $1,000,000 mark. I guarantee that our old neighbors had no clue what our net worth was. We showed no outward evidence that we had that much money. Some of those folks living in high-end homes, driving exotic cars, and living lavish lifestyles may well have net worth totals of *less than yours*.

Are there some true millionaires who *do* have some of the fancier trappings of life, including big homes and exotic cars? Yes, but most of them didn't acquire those fancy trappings until well after they had built their initial wealth.

What's the point of "Wheels of Fortune?" You become a millionaire by studying what millionaires do and then doing the same things yourself. Here's your list of what millionaires typically do when it comes to cars:

## ACTION STEPS

1. Buy gently used cars with low mileage that are in great shape.
2. Pay cash for them if possible.
3. Keep and use the car(s) until they are ready to fall apart.
4. Use the money you save to build your *real* fortune!

# Where's the Beef?

## It's not yoga, but you'll love to bend and stretch.

This game is really called "Bend and Stretch," but I had to change the title so it would fit alphabetically after "Wheels of Fortune," since the two games really tie in to each other. So just pretend the title is "Bend and Stretch," okay? Humor me.

Did you realize that grocery chains go to a great deal of trouble to help you spend as much money as possible in their stores? Well, of course they do! They want to make profits on their businesses, just as you do on yours. And what's the easiest way to make a profit in a grocery store? Putting your highest-margin items where they are easiest for the consumers to reach. I'm not kidding. Test this out the next time you visit your favorite grocery store. I've tried this test so many times you wouldn't believe it, and then I kept trying it because *I* didn't believe it, but now I'm convinced it's true.

Take a pocket calculator with you to the store, unless your store happens to be one of the few that actually posts the cost per ounce of all its selections. What will you find? The highest-cost-per-ounce items are right between waist level and shoulder level—the easiest space for you to reach! No bending or stretching required.

Do you want the lower-cost versions of the same products? You will very likely have to bend to get the size that's on the bottom shelf or stretch to get the one on the very top shelf. The store will never make it easy for you to reach the best bargain. Where will the generic items be? You can bet they'll be on the bottom shelf.

Moreover, don't make the mistake of thinking that a bigger size equates to "economy" size. Most of us are conditioned to believe that if we buy an item in bulk or in a larger size, it will cost less per ounce than its smaller counterpart will. But sometimes the smaller size is actually the better deal! Be aware and alert. Look at the prices on all the brands in all the sizes, high shelves and low, before making your selections.

Are you ready to widen your eyes a bit more? Then listen to this information I heard recently on the evening news. I was vacationing in Arizona, and a local Phoenix channel had done a survey of multiple stores within two discount chains. Not, mind you, to see which discount chain was the least expensive, but to compare the stores *within* each chain to see if the pricing was the same from store to store.

What was the surprising conclusion? Just because a store's name ends in "mart" doesn't mean its prices are identical in all of the other stores of that name. Even more amazing was the conclusion that the store prices in the neighborhoods with the highest annual incomes were significantly lower than the prices for the same common items in the neighborhoods with lower income levels. That just plain made me mad. On the other hand, it also made me determined that from now on, I'm heading for the stores in the wealthy neighborhoods. Why should I care if my old Explorer is next to brand new Mercedes and Jaguars? They won't remember me anyway. My money is just as green.

It helps to be educated. Bend and stretch. Learn to reach for the bargains, and park your Ford Explorer right next to that Mercedes in the rich neighborhood. Then put a great big smile on your face. You will be the one saving the money. *You* will be the millionaire next door!

## ACTION STEPS

When you are ready to go grocery shopping:

1. Make a list of all the items you need to purchase.

2. Find a handheld calculator to take with you.

3. Drive your car over to a grocery store in a wealthier neighborhood nearby.

4. Once in the store, be sure to check for variations of each product on the top and bottom shelves. The better values are generally harder to reach.

5. Don't assume that larger is less expensive. Use your calculator if necessary to be certain you are choosing the product that has the lowest cost per ounce. Sometimes the smaller size is actually the better deal.

6. Use great discipline in sticking to the items on your list. In particular, watch out for the items placed at the ends of each aisle in the store. That's where many stores put the "impulse" items. Unbelievably, sometimes those same items in their regular spots are less expensive than the ones on the ends! Beware.

7. Bend and stretch—that's the key. Reach a little and save a bundle.

# THINKING GAMES

# Opsticles

## No matter how dire your circumstances ...

For the title of this game, I've borrowed a word mentioned by author and speaker Wayne Dyer. If I remember the story correctly, when one of his daughters was young, she could never correctly pronounce the word "obstacles." When she tried to say it, it always came out as "opsticles," as if she were trying to rhyme it with "Popsicles."

To me, "opsticles" could be a clever combination of the words "optical" and "obstacle." By combining the two meanings, I arrived at a new definition: the choices we have about how to view the circumstances that present themselves in our lives. People often refer to life as a voyage. Interestingly, God doesn't give us any choice in advance about the vessels we sail in (our bodies) or what the weather will be like (the joys, obstacles, and circumstances that confront us and often arrive unannounced).

Let's talk a bit about the obstacles. In finance, there are many obstacles that can and often do confront us:

- Lack of money;
- Lack of knowledge;
- Unpredictable movements of the stock market and other investments;
- Unexpected "disasters" such as the loss of a job, an unexpected illness, a natural disaster like an earthquake, tornado, or hurricane, and the deaths of loved ones, especially primary breadwinners;
- Outliving our resources.

Not all of these disasters can be prevented, but there are many choices we can make that will at least lessen their impacts. We can:

- save money;
- gain knowledge;
- have diverse investments;
- have adequate homeowner's insurance, medical insurance, long-term care insurance, disability insurance, and life insurance;

- wisely use our resources during retirement so we can maximize the money we have (including, perhaps, annuities—streams of income that cannot be outlived).

The other thing we have control over is the way in which we choose to view the tougher circumstances that come our way. Let's face it—all of us have challenges, and some of those challenges could potentially lead to financial devastation if we haven't adequately prepared ourselves. Have you ever set your goals, made your plans, and started moving forward, only to find that some unexpected "opsticle" has reared its ugly head? We have, plenty of times! We've had deaths in the family, personal illnesses, personal injuries, and job layoffs (after twenty-eight years!). Other "opsticles" have included annual drops in income of as much as $40,000, $70,000, and $143,000 and losses in investments of $35,000, $39,000, and $44,000 over time periods as short as one or two weeks.

Some "opsticles" have been as brief as a day, and some have lasted two years or more. Those "opsticles" easily could have led us to devastation and despair. Why didn't they? Because we were prepared with cash reserves, excellent insurance, and a determination not to quit in spite of the setbacks. More importantly, however, we made deliberate decisions about how to "view" each of those apparent setbacks.

We believe that everything God allows into our lives is there for a purpose, usually to help us learn and grow. Did we learn and grow? Yes. We learned patience, gratitude, forbearance, and trust. We believe that God is ultimately in control of our finances. This was evidenced to us when one of our salaries was unexpectedly cut by $40,000. That same year was the first year that our investments made more than the entire salary was *before* it was cut. The employer didn't control our ultimate income for the year—God did.

Do you need to have a spiritual belief about money like we do? No, although I hope you do. Regardless of your personal beliefs, certain truths still remain.

- Life brings change and struggle.

- To get where we want to go, we must occasionally take detours.

- Action—moving forward in a positive way with all the energy we can muster—is frequently all that will get us out of our unfortunate circumstances.

- We always have choices about how to view our problems. We also have choices about how to respond.

We knew what our goals were; those didn't change. But the easy way to get to them disappeared—you might say that the highway was blocked—and we had to find ways to our goals using the surface streets and slower roads.

Were we always happy with our circumstances? No, we weren't. We did remember, though, that even if we can't always control our circumstances, we *can* control our thoughts, our actions, and our openness to learning and growing. Sometimes we had to take small steps—very small steps—but we kept moving forward in the direction of our goals and dreams. We might have been delayed, but we were still headed toward our destinations. You can be too.

## ACTION STEPS

1. Choose to take a positive approach. No matter how dire your circumstances, you always have a choice about how you respond mentally. Look for the lessons you can learn. Look for the wisdom you can gain. Someday you will be able to share that wisdom with others.

2. Take action. When faced with obstacles, no action is too small, but the more substantial your actions, the more impact they will have. Taking action will help lessen your anxiety.

3. Remember: this too shall pass. Always keep your long-range goals firmly planted in your mind. Knowing your ultimate destination will help you readjust your direction when you get temporarily blown off course.

4. There will always be some things we cannot control. Accept those for what they are and look for the things you *can* control. That's where your actions will have impact.

# Pelican

**At least I recognize my neuroses ... and I'm sure my new medications will help.**

One day I was sitting on the balcony of one of my favorite beach hotels, over-looking the Pacific Ocean, when I happened to see a large number of good-sized birds circling and diving into the ocean some distance off the beach. Birds fascinate me, so I went into my hotel room and picked up the binoculars I travel with for just such occasions. What I saw through the binoculars turned out to be a double surprise. The birds were pelicans—it was the first time I'd seen them from that location, not to mention in such numbers (there were at least fifty!)—and there were also whales! *Wow!!* What an incredible experience, seeing several whales breaching and blowing and simultaneously watching the pelicans circling and diving into the ocean with great splashes.

You would be correct if you guessed that I do not know much about either species, but I did put together a couple of guesses about what was going on. First, I assumed that whales needed to eat a *lot* of food and that they probably tended to assemble in areas where plenty of food was available. Secondly, I assumed that pelicans also liked to eat and that they surely knew that anywhere they could spot a whale, there was likely to be plenty of food. They are smart birds, those pelicans!

Then, since I think about money a lot (the more you think about something, the more it is attracted to your life), I just naturally wondered if there was a lesson I could learn from what I was observing. Yes, I decided, there was.

In the investment world, there are a few really big hitters (Warren Buffet and others like him, i.e. the whales) and plenty of us smaller hitters (pelicans). I decided that just like the pelicans searching for whales to learn where the food was, we human pelicans could do something similar. No, I can't walk right up to Warren Buffet and ask him for investment advice. However, I *can* go to the library, check out any number of excellent books written by the "whales" of the investment world, and learn about how they spot the "food," and so can you.

Being the excessively analytical person that I am, I've been tracking the number of books I read each year for more than twenty years now. Each year, *some* of the books I read relate to finance and investing. One day this past year, I started wondering if there was any correlation between the number of financial books I'd read each year and the amount of increase in my wealth in each of those years. It seemed like a bit of a stretch, but I was curious.

Well, guess what? I made an Excel spreadsheet and graphed the number of financial books I'd read each year. Then I went back and overlaid that chart with the year-to-year increases in my net worth. It was shocking. The two charts mirrored each other almost perfectly!

Yes, I'll admit that I'm pretty weird for thinking about and making a chart like that. (At least I recognize my neuroses ... and I'm sure my new medications will help.) But the fact remains that there was, in fact, a high correlation over a twenty-year period between the number of financial books I'd read (the wisdom I was gaining) and the relative increases in my net worth.

With lightning-bolt clarity, the painfully obvious smacked me upside the head: I needed to increase the number of financial books I read each year! Obviously, the more time I spend "in the presence of the whales"—albeit through the books they have written—the more food I find.

Want more money? Read more books. Think like a pelican.

## ACTION STEPS

1.  Decide to make a study of the financial "whales"—that is, those people who have made and successfully invested large amounts of money.

2.  Read every book and article you can find by or about those successful investors.

3.  Keep written summaries of what you have learned.

4.  Review your summaries on a regular basis and see what similar (if smaller) steps you can take with your own money.

5.  See the references section at the back of the book for a list of some of the financial books I've enjoyed and visit www.wordsofabundance.com for some further bits of wisdom.

# The "I" Exam

## How to make your own diagnosis, plan your treatment, and get better.

No, it's not like playing doctor. This is a game you play by yourself. Well, at least initially. You may want to involve your spouse and/or significant other at some point, but for now, this is really about *you*. Like seeing a doctor, however, this game does involve asking and answering a list of questions in order to make a diagnosis, chart a course of treatment, and get better!

Here are the "I" questions to ask and answer:

- Am I currently unhappy with my finances? (If you answer "yes," then also ask yourself why.)

- What do I really want?

- What are my financial goals?

- How much money do I want to have, and by when? (Answer for one month, one year, five years, ten years, retirement age, and any other time period that might be significant for you.)

- Have I set intermediate steps in order to track my progress?

- Am I making daily progress and moving forward?

- What can I do, starting today, that will cause me to be happier with my answers to the first five questions if I ask them again a month from today?

Saving money is part of the larger puzzle of your life. It's nice to save money, but why do you want to? If you have big, exciting reasons for saving, you will be much more motivated to use these games and actually move forward. Sometimes the real reason we haven't saved money is that we haven't taken the time to decide why we want to *have* money saved to begin with. Answering these questions about why you want money, how much money you want, and by what date you want to have it may be all it takes to get you moving. If you have enough reasons to want to save, the methods will be the easy part.

Next, put your answers and your goals in writing. Hold them at arm's length from your eyes. If you can clearly "see" what you want, you have successfully passed your "I" exam.

PS: One last thing, though it may seem unrelated at first. Add one final question to your list: "What are the 'open loops' in my life?" Open loops are projects you have started but not finished, things that are on your "to do" list but keep getting postponed, etc. They are the distractions that keep you from being truly focused.

Once you have identified them, close as many of your open loops as possible, or else take them off your "to do" list and put them on a "someday/maybe" list. Having too many open loops is like continuously looking through a kaleidoscope. There are lots of pretty colors and interesting images, but nothing is ever truly in focus. Narrow your "to do" list to as few items as possible. Truly answer the question, "What matters most?" Be sure the answers to that question are reflected in your goals and your action plans. Money flows more easily when you have clarity and focus.

## ACTION STEPS

1. Work toward gaining clarity and focus about your money.

2. Put your goals in writing.

3. Spend time every day reviewing your goals and monitoring the steps you've taken toward those goals.

4. Look for the open loops in your life that you can either close or put on a "someday/maybe" list so that they are off your mind for now.

5. Pinpoint what matters most with regard to your money and begin living and acting in ways that are in tune with that answer.

# THE WEATHER GAME

# Winter

**Getting your "donkey" out of Dodge before the snow flies.**

If you live in Minnesota (or pretty much *any* of the northern states or countries), what predictably follows spring, summer, and fall? Very good: winter! Unless you love high heating bills, shoveling snow until your back hurts, and getting frostbite on your fingers, toes, and ears, you may want to consider a warmer climate as a refuge for the season.

There is a word in the dictionary for a person who is stupid, silly, or a fool. In case you haven't figured out the exact word, it also can mean any of a number of horselike perissodactylous mammals (family *Equidae*) that have long ears and short manes. Are you still not with me? Try a vulgar, slang word for buttocks. It is a three-letter word that starts with "A" and ends with "S" and has another "S" in the middle.

Okay. Now that we've agreed on the animal in question, when the winter comes, wouldn't you want to get that animal out of Dodge and down to Phoenix before the snow flies? If you know you will be facing winter and can't move to Arizona for the duration, you would at least take some steps to be ready, right? It's likely that you would take the following actions:

- Ensure that your residence is well insulated.
- Be certain that you have plenty of fuel for warmth.
- Purchase a snowblower or hire the neighbor's kid for snow removal.
- Check that your car battery is in good shape.
- Put your snow tires on.
- Check your antifreeze.
- Get out your long underwear, down coat, gloves, scarves, and insulated boots.

What I'm getting at here is the fact that economic and financial conditions change, and a prudent person will understand and prepare for those changes in a similar manner to how you might prepare for winter. Whatever the current state of financial affairs in your beloved country (inflation, deflation, expansion, contraction, war or peace, growth or recession), like the seasons, things are going to change. The wise will consider the implications of change, whether economic, social, political, technological, or military, and prepare as best they can in advance.

So what exactly can you do? Here are some brief suggestions.

- Read, think, and research how various forms of investments have been impacted in past times of change.

- Ask yourself at any given moment, "Is my money in the best place? What investments are unpopular at the moment that I can buy at bargain prices?"

- Take appropriate action. If you need to move existing money, do so. If you have excess investable cash, look for the "sale" signs. What are the investments no one wants right now? Snatch them up! Buy cheap.

- Skip ahead and read the chapter on lemmings. No matter what the current investment climate, you can bet that the majority of your friends and family are heading in exactly the wrong direction. Watch where they are going, and give serious thought to taking the opposite track.

- Do not buy all at once or put all your money into one investment. Keep some cash reserves so that you are ready for future opportunities as they arrive. Stay well diversified, knowing that your crystal ball may be imperfect.

- Keep at least a small percentage of your money in the "disaster" investments: gold, silver, quality gold stocks, energy stocks, and (only if you are knowledgeable) perhaps foreign currency.

- Start preparing now. Spring, summer, and fall are excellent times to be looking ahead and getting ready for winter. As in those northern climates, you never know when the first snow will fall. Be ready in advance.

## ACTION STEPS

1. Protect what you have. The base of your investment pyramid is the hardest to build. Once it is in place, be certain that money stays in stable, conservative, well-protected places.

2. Study the writings of the doomsayers. Plenty of books are out there predicting economic chaos, depression, and bad years. Whether the authors are accurate in their predictions or not, you can still gain valuable insights into preparing yourself for all possible economic weather conditions.

3. Do your best to ignore your emotions. There is extreme temptation to follow the euphoria of the crowd, but hold fast. Take a hard look at the investments that no one currently wants. There's nothing quite as satisfying as buying a

solid investment "on sale" when no one wants it, then selling it when the crowd really wants it.

4. Take your time making decisions. Do your research thoroughly. Know what you are buying and why.

5. Stay diversified. With enough flowers in the garden, something will always be blooming.

6. Keep some cash reserves.

7. Remember that the seasons inevitably progress from one to the next. Be wise. Prepare for winter while it is still summer. Summer can be short. Don't procrastinate.

# THE "NO-NO" GAMES

This section is devoted to the games your poor neighbors play. Let's face it: You have some poor neighbors. They don't *look* poor, but trust me, they are. They may have fancy houses, fine cars, speedboats, more shoes than you, or any of a million other things you envy, but the odds are exceptionally high that the reason they have those things is that they are deeply in debt. They may have very high mortgages, maxed-out credit cards, home equity loans, and money owed to friends or family. This is *not* the way to wealth.

In each no-no game, I've tried to identify a poor financial habit or poor financial decision and then to show you "the better way." Sometimes the no-no will be brief and the better way will take up the bigger portion of the description. Regardless, it is important to know what *not* to do and how to become one of the few who are acting from wisdom rather than foolishness. You'll easily see the foolishness in these remaining games, so I'll spend more time showing you how to be wise instead.

The truly wise learn from the mistakes of others. Since you don't have nearly enough time to make all these financial mistakes on your own, here's your chance to profit from the folly of your neighbors and to make better decisions for yourself.

Enjoy!

# Bondage

**Are you jealous of the neighbor with the nicer house, the nicer car, and the bigger swimming pool? Here's how to get the sweetest revenge.**

Wow, we're going to talk about bondage? No, no—I'm not talking about the kinky neighbors two blocks over. I'm talking about *financial* bondage. How do people get into financial bondage? They:

- incur a small amount of short-term debt;
- incur more short-term debt;
- incur longer-term debt;
- get a debt-consolidation loan;
- realize they have more room available on their credit cards again due to their consolidation loan, go back to the first step, and repeat the process.

Why would people do this? Four reasons come to mind:

1. We live in a consumer-based society that constantly bombards us with advertisements for things that will make us happier and prettier, give us more prestige, take away our wrinkles, and so on.

2. "I want it, and I want it now," that is, greed.

3. They lack discipline. "I want it, I want it now, and I want it before my neighbor gets it!"

4. They fail to delay gratification. "I want it, I want it now, I have room on my credit cards, and therefore I can buy it now. HA!"

Here's a sample scenario. Neighbor one buys a Ford Explorer. Neighbor two buys a Ford Explorer, Eddie Bauer edition. Neighbor one then buys a Ford Explorer, Eddie Bauer edition, and adds $2,000 custom wheels. Neighbor two then buys an Explorer, Eddie Bauer edition, with custom wheels, and adds dual DVD players for the kids in the backseats.

Now what does neighbor one do? Better go for a Lexus this time—the new hybrid one. Ah, but then neighbor two gets the hybrid Lexus and adds the $2,500 oversized chrome wheels, of course. The cycle just continues without end.

Who wins this game? It certainly isn't either of the neighbors. The only winners I can think of are the car dealers and the companies who are financing all this madness. So stop the vicious cycle. Let the neighbor *have* the nicer car. You are going to be *richer*—won't that be wonderful revenge?

## ACTION STEPS

1. Understand how people get into financial bondage.
2. Decide that you are not going to be one of those people.
3. If you are already in financial bondage, start new habits immediately and begin working your way toward financial freedom.
4. If you aren't in financial bondage, pat yourself on the back and continue on the road to wealth.

# Bric-a-Brac and Beyond

## How did we get from mix-it-yourself, frozen orange juice to certified organic, 100 percent pure pomegranate juice and homemade smoothies?

Bric-a-brac is an old-fashioned term for knickknacks—small, ornamental objects that you place around a room for decoration. Almost all of us have knickknacks. Have you ever noticed, however, that you've gradually replaced your simple, inexpensive knickknacks with objects that are more ornate, rarer, more exquisite, and yes, more expensive? What happened? What's happened is that you've moved from amenities (things which add to your comfort and convenience) to outright luxuries (the best and most costly things that offer the most physical comfort and satisfaction).

Here's an example that will be hard for you younger readers to believe. There was a time in my life when my parents owned just one television ... and it had a black and white picture! Then one day, right around World Series time, all of a sudden it was replaced with a *color* television. (The green grass on the field was entirely amazing!) Each year or two, the color television kept getting larger.

Now we interrupt our story for a commercial break while I grow up and move away from home.

(Commercial) Announcer: "Isn't this a great book? There are a *lot* of people you know who could really use these games, aren't there? Do them a favor and buy them each their own copy of *Money Games!* No, better yet, encourage them to buy their own copies. You will save your own money, and they will place more value on something they had to purchase for themselves. Aren't you the clever one? HA!"

(After the commercial break.) So now I was out on my own and had my own home. (This is still a lot of years ago!) If Mom and Dad had a color television, it seemed only right that my bride and I should have a color television as well. Therefore, we bought one. We put it in the living room. Then it seemed only right that we should also have one in the "breakfast nook" (one end of the kitchen). After all, everyone else did. Then, somehow, we needed a color television in the bedroom! We stopped before putting them in the bathrooms, but eventually we had four color televisions plus a portable black and white, and just two of us lived in the house. Hmm. Of course, we've learned our lesson since then. Now we have a bigger house but only two televisions. But did I mention that the televisions are *huge* and that they are high definition?

Have we really learned our lesson? Yeah, right. I can already picture our next home with its private home theater, THX surround sound, and plush, reclining chairs. (I can also imagine the live-in maid to bring us our beverages and popcorn.)

What's happening to us has likely been happening to you as well. Many of us experience that subtle shift from amenities to luxuries, from simple and inexpensive to state of the art and expensive.

Let's look at some other examples. Have you gone from ...

- … drinking tap water to bottled water to Perrier? Maybe you should purchase a water filtration system for the entire house! After all, you might need purified drinking water in the bathtub some night. Who knows?

- … one VHS tape player (does anybody still remember those?) and sixty video tapes to four VHS players and three hundred video tapes? Then did you upgrade to a single DVD player with sixty DVDs, then to multiple DVD players with five hundred DVDs, then to high-definition DVD players with a collection of high-definition DVDs?

- … a used Volkswagen Beetle to a small SUV (new, of course), to a large SUV, then to adding a chrome-laden custom chopper and a luxurious BMW alongside, then to ditching the gas-guzzling SUV in favor of a hybrid decked-out Lexus?[34]

- … a used set of skis to new skis, then to multiple pairs of skis, and finally to multiple pairs of skis plus snowmobiles and snowboards?

- … playing "Pong" on your computer[35] to EA Sports on your computer (several consecutive upgraded versions), then to a separate Playstation® plus computer games, then to multiple Playstation® IIs plus games on multiple computers, then to waiting countless hours in line for PS3® the day it came out, to ... whatever came next? I admit to being behind the curve on this one.

- … a television that got three or four local channels to one that gets more than nine hundred channels via satellite or cable?

---

[34] All of which are, of course, parked outside your three-car garage; the garage is filled with "stuff" that won't fit in the house. Now you have the expensive toys outside in the driveway while the nearly worthless stuff is protected in the garage. Wow. Do you really??

[35] Okay, so most of you aren't old enough to remember Pong. I'm *old*, all right?

- … a television that showed one channel at a time to one with picture in picture, then to the high-definition package that lets you see up to eight football games simultaneously?

- … an eight-hundred-square-foot condominium to a four thousand-plus-square-foot home just for the two of you? (Ouch. Guilty.)

- … cleaning your home yourself to hiring a team of three or four cleaning ladies to "spiff it up" once a week?

- … doing your own wash to sending it all out to the dry cleaners?

- … wearing perfume or cologne that could be purchased at the drugstore to designer fragrances and cosmetics?

- … paperback books to hardbacks to an Amazon Kindle®?

- … a few books to a full-size bookcase full of books, then to several bookcases full of books, then to bookcases overflowing with books in nearly every room of the house? Did you finally have to build a five-thousand-volume custom library with solid mahogany shelves and a hidden secret room?

- … home-brewed coffee to Starbucks venti mocha nonfat double shot with whip?

- … going on walks in the neighborhood for exercise to walks in the neighborhood with wrist and ankle weights, then to walking with an iPod, then to the membership in the twenty-four-hour fitness club? Then did you get your own recumbent Exercycle for home use, then an elliptical trainer for home use, then your own complete home gym, then a personal trainer to go with your home gym?

- … renting golf clubs at the public golf course to owning your own set of used clubs, then to new clubs, then to Calloway clubs and a membership at the public course, then to Calloway clubs plus your own golf cart and a lifetime membership at the country club?

- … bowling at the local bowling alley to owning your own personalized bowling shoes, then to your own monogrammed bowling ball and bowling gloves with a custom case? (You're not serious, right?)

Do those transitions sound a bit outlandish? Well, yes, that's a fairly extreme list. However, my bet is that if you are an American consumer, there are at least two or three things on that list that hit close to home. I bet you've progressed at least part way down some of them.

Mentally back up with me for a moment. Are you really healthier drinking Perrier instead of tap water? (No, you don't need to send me the scientific studies.) Can you get from home to work any faster in rush hour in your hybrid than you did in your Volkswagen? (By the way, are you aware that having a car—any car—is a luxury that 92 percent of the world's population never enjoys?) Are you really any more fit now that you have your complete home gym than you were when you worked out elsewhere?

How did we get from mix-it-yourself frozen orange juice to certified organic, 100 percent pure pomegranate juice and homemade smoothies? How did we go from home-brewed Folgers coffee to Starbucks and individual serving Senseo coffee pods?

How many luxury items have *you* let become necessities? Have you thought about how much it costs to maintain and store all those items? (Your $30,000 car is sitting outside in the elements while *what* is in the garage?)

Let's ask a few more questions.

- How many things do you own that seemed like such great ideas at the time but now serve only to collect dust, thereby keeping the cleaning ladies employed?

- When is the last time you actually *used* your electric shoe polisher? Did you *ever* actually use it? (Okay, so you tried it once.)

- Are there other items you have you purchased and used only once or only a few times? Do you still have them?

Wouldn't this be a great time to ask two more simple questions?

1) Why?

2) How much more money would you have to invest and add to your real wealth if you scaled back some luxuries to simple amenities?

## ACTION STEPS

1. Look around your home and see how many items you can list that are rare, ornate, exquisite, or just downright expensive.

2. From that list, make marks beside any that are upgrades from similar items available at much lower costs.

3. Evaluate whether the expensive luxuries are really worth the extra money you are paying for them.

4. Break with conventional wisdom (and the neighbors) and boldly go where almost no one goes anymore—to the drugstore for cosmetics and perfume/cologne. (Gasp!)

5. See how much money you can save by buying fewer and less expensive versions of your normal consumables.

6. Invest the saved money and smile. You are on your way to real wealth!

# Holiday

**Thank goodness you have plastic. If you were carrying cash, you'd have to go back to the bank.**

There was an estimate in 2006 that "people" (I guess that would be "Americans") were going to spend more than $120 billion using their credit cards between Thanksgiving and Christmas. I don't know what the actual total ended up being, but if that number is even close, we have to get in on some of that action. Just think what we could buy with that much money ... and what some of us *did* buy with those nifty plastic cards! Credit cards were *meant* for holidays, right? After all, think of all the advantages of using them.

- You often get an interest-free grace period.
- You are building your credit worthiness.
- You may be able to get additional discounts.
- You might get rewards such as rebates and other benefits.
- You may get free purchase protection on your purchases. (Even though you haven't a clue what that means, it sounds good!)
- You may get free extended warranties (that you'll forget about by the time you need them, but they're free, so why not?)
- You don't have to worry about your cash being stolen because you won't be carrying any!

Does it matter how much you buy? No, of course it doesn't matter. You'll have all next year to pay them off, and if you just make minimum payments, you could have *years* to pay it all back. Those credit card companies are so generous ... and right at the time of year that we need them most. That's awesome.

Let's say you want to buy your wife a new sixty-inch plasma TV. (You know she'll really appreciate it when football season rolls around.) Maybe your budget for the TV is $1,000, but you just happen to find a *spectacular* one (original price $6,000) on sale half-price for $3,000. Now, who could pass up a deal like that?

Thank goodness you have plastic. If you were carrying cash, you'd have to go back to the bank. That would be a complete bummer. Someone else might buy the last one before you got back to the store.

Let's talk about shopping rules.

**Rule 1**: Don't even worry about a plan. When you find just the right brooch for Aunt Bea, whom you met only once ten years ago but will see at the family celebration this year, you need to be ready to snap it up! The only plan you need is to carry all your credit cards with you in case one or two get maxed out.

**Rule 2**: The average person will spend about $1,000 on holiday gifts. Remember, though, that you are not an average person. It's the amount you spend that counts, not whether or not anyone really likes the gifts you give.

**Rule 3**: Don't even worry about the size of the bill you'll get in January. Odds are that you'll get some 0 percent credit card offers near the beginning of the year, and you can just put off paying for those gifts until later. After all, you'll need your money for all those January white sales and to stock up on the half-off Christmas items you'll want for next year.

**Rule 4**: Make a list of the people for whom you need to buy gifts. Without a list, you may not remember some very important people. For example, did you remember ...

- ... your hairstylist?
- ... your manicurist?
- ... your broker?
- ... the garbage man?
- ... all your kids' teachers?
- ... the mailman?
- ... your boss?
- ... all your coworkers?
- ... all seventy of your direct reports (team members)?
- ... the janitor?
- ... the preacher?
- ... the preacher's wife?
- ... the choir director?
- ... the funeral director and priest/minister who helped everyone say good-bye to Aunt Ethel?
- ... your favorite cocktail hostess?
- ... your favorite bartender?
- ... your favorite waiter and waitress?
- ... your gardener?

- … your cleaning ladies?
- … your handyman?
- … the dry cleaner?
- … the vacuum repair guy?
- … the plumber?
- … the butcher?
- … the baker?
- … the candlestick maker (just kidding)?

Well, you get the idea. You have a lot of shopping to do. Better make a list. If you're compulsive, you can always make the list on your computer so you won't have to start from scratch next year. Make your list and stick to it.

**Rule 5**: Carry the list with you all year. You always get the best selection when each new season's products first come out. You'll get the best pick of sizes and colors that way.

**Rule 6**: Apply for every credit card offer you get all year. Yes, apply for *all* of them. You can never have too much credit when it comes to holiday shopping!

## ACTION STEPS

1. Realize that all the above was a no-no game. These are *not* things you want to do. (Some of your friends and neighbors will, but don't you even think about doing them if you want to be wealthy.)

2. Abide by a different set of rules:

   a. Do have a plan. However, it should be one that has not only the names of your intended gift recipients but also the limit that you plan to spend on each.

   b. Never go over your budgeted amount just because you have a credit card rather than cash.

3. It's more important to know your holiday spending limit and stick to it than to spend as much as you can on specific individuals. If you get an unexpected bargain for one recipient, it might be acceptable to go a little over on another, but keep the total budget clearly in mind.

4. When you are deciding on your spending limit, think about how much cash you will have available in January to pay the bills in full. Don't buy more expensive gifts with your credit card than you would have with cash.

5. It is okay to use the same list from year to year, but revisions are necessary. Do carry it with you all year if you like, but look for *sales* on the items you have in mind.

6. Play "chicken" with your credit card companies. Call each one and ask for a special holiday offer. Ask for 0 percent on purchases for six months, and if they won't do it, tell them you'll be using another company's credit card this year that will give you that deal. Don't plan to actually use the 0 percent for six months, but if for some reason you have an unexpected credit crunch in January, it will buy you some extra time.

7. Watch for deals from department stores. Many offer discounts of 10 and 15 percent if you buy items using their cards. Use those cards for the discounts and then immediately transfer the balances to your lower-rate credit cards before any interest is charged.

8. Have the money set aside to pay all your credit card bills in full once they arrive. If you've stuck to your budget and planned ahead, you'll be all set.

Happy holidays!

# L.A. Story

**And why the heck don't you do something about those nasty wrinkles around your eyes?**

Have you seen the movie *L.A. Story* with Steve Martin? One of my favorite scenes from that movie is when Steve's character gets in his car, backs out of his driveway, drives next door, parks, and gets out ... to visit his neighbor.

That's quintessential Los Angeles. Buy it, flaunt it. Take the easy way out. Live for today; tomorrow we may be nuked. Never mind about the other guy. You had better grab your own share of the gusto.

Ah, yes, California. The land where bigger is better.

Like chests, for example.

What?

You need bigger *pirate* chests to hold all your loot! What did you think I meant?

It's the mentality of "I'm driving the really big Hummer because I can afford to buy it and I really don't care how much gas costs. So there, buddy. That means I'm smarter, wealthier, and just plain better than you are. Want to make something of it?"

It's the mentality of "Yeah, I bought a five-carat diamond just to prove they come that big, and also to celebrate my successful facelift and tummy tuck. What's that microscopic thing on *your* finger? And why the heck don't you do something about those nasty wrinkles around your eyes?"

It is a world where nothing is ever big enough, expensive enough, flashy enough, or impressive enough. Do you know anybody who thinks like that? Do *you* think like that?

Obviously I'm poking fun at Los Angeles. I can—I live there. Nevertheless, you can find those attitudes just about anywhere.

A few years ago I was reading *The Sigma Protocol* by the late author Robert Ludlum.[36] In it was a paragraph that hit me right between the eyes. Bear in mind that the book was written some years ago, but if you adjust the prices for today's economy, the point is still powerful. Here's the quote:

---

[36] Ludlum, Robert. *The Sigma Protocol.* New York: St. Martin's Press, 2001.

"When you buy a bottle of Dom Perignon, you have spent a sum of money that could have vaccinated a village in Bangladesh, spared lives from the ravages of disease.... Can you deny that the ninety dollars a bottle of Dom Perignon costs could have easily saved half a dozen lives, perhaps more? Think about it. The bottle will yield seven or eight glasses of wine. Each glass, we can say, represents a life lost."

I don't know if that analogy is accurate or not, but it certainly made me take pause. Where are we going with our conspicuous consumption, and at what cost to humankind and planet Earth? Will you be one of those who says, "Enough is enough!" and begins sharing even a small portion of your bounty with those who are less fortunate? You never know—in the next life, roles could be reversed. What would it be like if *you* were the bedraggled person with the "Will work for food" sign and the former bedraggled person took your place? If that person decides to act just as you act toward the less fortunate now, will you be happy or sad? Would you be fed or continue to go hungry?

Remember the tattered man sitting outside the gas station last week? You know, the one you ignored and walked right past even though you clearly heard his request for money. What if he treats you that way when he's playing your role and you are playing his? Will you be as forgiving as he was? (He didn't berate you for ignoring him, did he?)

Take time to reflect. How many times have you ignored a simple request for help when it was within your power to *be* of help? Will you continue to ignore those pleas? Are there times when you come pretty close to driving next door to see the neighbor? How many times have you driven somewhere you could have walked, taken a bus, or bicycled? How many times have you driven alone when you could have carpooled? Just how many pairs of shoes do you really need? Life is choice. Choose wisely; give when you have the opportunity.

ACTION STEPS (The No-No Version)

1. Rent and watch the movie *L.A. Story*, starring Steve Martin.

2. Pretend you are in California.

3. Get a bigger chest.

4. Ignore anyone who requests your help, financial or otherwise, and hoard all you can for yourself.

OR TAKE THE HIGHER ROAD:

1. Rent and watch the movie *L.A. Story*, starring Steve Martin.
2. Pretend you are in California.
3. Decide you will rebel against the "counter" culture (as in jewelry counter, clothing counter, and "bling" counter) of spend, spend, spend.
4. Give when you have the opportunity.
5. Remember that some day, roles could easily be reversed. What goes around comes around. What will you want coming around?

# Lemmings

## Are you in line, following along?

The next game your financially challenged neighbors are very likely playing is one I call "Lemmings." What are lemmings? Lemmings are small rodents usually found in or near the Arctic. They usually weigh one to four ounces and are three to six inches long. They have very short tails and long, soft fur.

What do lemmings do? The myth is that they blindly follow each other everywhere, even off of cliffs! Although that myth has apparently been proven false, it has still become a metaphor for the way crowds of people behave when they foolishly follow each other regardless of the consequences.

Are you in line, following along? If you have a low savings rate, misuse your credit cards, and/or are substantially in debt, you may unknowingly have a compound last name—like Randall Lemming-Petrick, for example.

Have you seen the recent studies on how much Americans are saving out of their total incomes? A variety of numbers have been in print, ranging from *negative* numbers (people spending more than they earn!) to very low numbers (2 or 3 percent). Most sources say it basically averages out to zero. The one thing you won't ever see in print is a *large* number. But there's a *precipice* out there, folks. The looming cliff is called retirement, and if you aren't saving well for it, you'll find yourself walking off the edge right along with your neighbors. Don't follow the crowd.

Yes, the masses are full of folly. Not only are they missing the boat on savings (as per above), they are also missing the boat with their credit cards. Maybe they are even *buying the boat* with their credit cards. That, of course, is the problem. We see our neighbors spending all they earn, and we buy stuff to keep up with them. High credit card debt (with its often-accompanying high interest rates) is a death knell for financial success.

Finally, how much long-term debt have you accumulated, and what do you have to show for it? If that money has gone toward purchasing depreciating assets like cars, motorcycles, boats, and other miscellaneous bling, ask yourself who you are trying to impress or keep up with. Is it worth sacrificing a bright financial future just to impress your friends or neighbors with your new "whozzi-whatzit?" If you give serious thought to that question, my guess is that your answer will be no.

Watch your friends and neighbors. Are they spending more than they earn? Are they running up debt on their credit cards? Are they buying depreciating assets and using debt to do it? If so, they are on a dangerous merry-go-round. They are going around and around and getting nowhere. Is that the destination you have in mind as well?

When the crowd is all going one way, take heed. Then give serious thought to going the opposite way. Make your own decisions, and make them positive for your financial future.

Let's spell it together: L-E-M-M-I-N-G. What does it spell? Disaster!

## ACTION STEPS

1. Realize that there is a natural tendency to want to be part of the crowd.
2. Take note that the crowd is generally wrong.
   - They generally aren't saving any money.
   - They have overextended themselves with debt, especially credit card debt.
   - They have used long-term debt to purchase depreciating assets.
3. Take heed of what the crowd is doing, and give serious thought to going in the opposite direction. After all, it sounds cool to be a "contrarian."

# Lemmings II
# (Also Known as "Gossip")

## Where are you getting your financial advice?

Next, let's talk about investing—another opportunity to join the Lemming family. The typical scenario is this: We hear about someone who's made a large profit on a particular stock, and we rush out to buy it too. One person buys Enron (oops, I did that) and raves about how much it's going up. (Gossip!) Then, of course, his neighbor has to rush out and buy Enron as well, and his neighbor, and so on down the rest of the block, including you. How many of those buyers do you think actually did any research on Enron? Would *you*? (I didn't.)

So what do most people do? They jump into the market at the peak of hysteria (the top) and sell in the depths of despondency (the bottom). Buying high and selling low is the exact opposite of what leads to success. Be sure you are not playing "Lemmings II" and blindly following along.

Where are you getting your financial advice? If your neighbor says, "Wow! I'm making a killing on Wha-ze-widget stock!," do you run right out and buy some yourself? After all, you think to yourself, if *she* says it's great, it must be, right? After all, *she's* driving a Lexus. It's obvious that she must be smarter than I am.

Have you heard of what is now called "The Tech Wreck?" There was a time not so many years ago that technology stocks were all the rage. Everyone who was anyone was buying technology stocks, and often after no more research than hearing a neighbor saying, "You should buy this—it's doing GREAT!" One person followed another person, who followed another person, and pretty soon everyone was doing the same thing: buying technology stocks at whatever price. The price didn't matter. What mattered was being one of the in-crowd who owned technology stocks.

What happened to that crowd? They all fell off the cliff together. Technology stocks crashed, and millions of people lost money—*lots* of money!

Everyone has perfect hindsight, of course. Moreover, everyone who lost money in the Tech Wreck now says, "I won't do that again." However, what exactly is it that they won't do again? Buy technology stocks? If that's their answer, they haven't learned the lesson. If their answer is "I won't follow the crowd," then rejoice with them because they are now wiser.

Take some time and think about whom you are following and emulating. If you listen to advice from others, do you look behind the curtain to see their real results? If you are going to follow someone's advice, look for someone who is living below his or her means and building solid financial structures.

It's your choice, of course, but if you are going to follow someone, why would you choose someone who is headed for the cliff's edge? Avoid blindly following gossip and hot tips from your neighbors.

Now, on the off chance that your neighbor is Warren Buffet, *call me!* We can *both* follow along. However, before we do, we'll go over and visit Warren's game room. If he has the stock pages taped up over his dartboard, we're out of there.

## ACTION STEPS

1. Find out if Warren Buffet is your neighbor.

2. If so, find out his favorite dessert and start providing him with a steady supply.

3. If not, consider moving ... or at the least consider ignoring any advice you get from your actual neighbors, unless:

   - your neighbor has a large and growing net worth;

   - your neighbor has no credit card debt;

   - your neighbor uses credit only to buy appreciating assets;

   - your neighbor is moving against the crowd and avoiding small rodents with short tails and long, soft fur.

# Monopoly (Diversification, Part I)

**You have the best chance of staying afloat if you have several different life rafts available.**

Here's another no-no game that some of your neighbors may be playing, though I hope you're not. This game is called "Monopoly," but it's not the same as the Milton Bradley version. In this game, the players often work for large, publicly traded companies and receive generous amounts of company stock. Sometimes the stock comes as a bonus, sometimes in the form of stock options, and sometimes even in the form of matching contributions to a 401(k) plan. If the company is doing well, these "gifts" can be wonderful! But here's the catch. (You knew there would be one, didn't you?) Employees of these companies often end up with all their eggs in one basket.

You know what they say about that, right? "Never put all your eggs in the same basket." Why do you suppose someone came up with that piece of advice? My guess is that it came from someone who *did* put all his eggs in one basket and then forgot to *be careful with the basket*! All is well as long as the company or corporation is doing well, but what happens to the basket if the company stock takes a big hit? Your eggs hit the ceramic tile floor. Ooh, what a mess. There goes your retirement money.

Every financial planner I know or have read about (and that's a bunch!) gives the same, one-word piece of advice: Diversify! What does that mean? Diversifying means that instead of having many eggs in *one* basket, you have a few eggs in each of *many* baskets (or at the least several baskets). Different kinds of investments go up or down in different ways. For example, if interest rates go up, rates on certificates of deposit and money market accounts also go up, but bond prices fall. If interest rates go down, just the opposite happens: CDs and money market accounts pay out less, and bond prices rise. If inflation rates are low or falling, precious metals tend to fall as well. If inflation is rising, precious metals tend to rise as well.

So what does all that mean, exactly? It just means that you have the best chance of staying afloat if you have several different life rafts available. If one raft has a leak, you'll survive by riding in one of the other ones. At any given time, some kinds of investments will be doing well and other kinds will be doing poorly. How do you know which investments will be the ones to do well? You don't. That's exactly why you need a variety of investments. If some of your investments are doing poorly, they will be balanced out by others that are doing well.

Be careful, though, not to fall into the trap of thinking that you are well diversified if you have growth mutual funds from Janus, Fidelity, and Vanguard. All three are still the same types of investments. You can invest in Janus, Fidelity, and Vanguard if you wish, but make sure you also have different kinds of funds: growth funds, balanced funds, international funds, bond funds, etc.

Need help? There are many excellent advisors who can help you with this process and many good reference books if you'd like to learn on your own.

What is the bottom line? Don't play monopoly unless you are playing the board game. There's a one-word secret you must know and practice. (From the way most of your neighbors act, it *must* be a secret!) The good news is that now it's not a secret to you. To you, it's knowledge. *Diversify!*

## ACTION STEPS

1. Spend at least fifteen minutes per day (just 1 percent of your time!) reading about and learning about investments.

2. Use your time to learn about the various kinds of investments available to you.

3. Plan your investing strategy in advance, before you have even saved the money to begin.

4. Once you begin investing even small amounts, spread your money among at least two or three different kinds of investments.

5. You've worked hard to accumulate the money you're investing, so protect those precious eggs. Never keep them all in just one basket. Diversify!

# Speeding (Diversification, Part II)

**Speed limits change from place to place and time to time, and your investments need to do the same.**

Have you ever traveled across the country by car? If so, did you notice that you can't just go seventy miles per hour the whole way? If you try going that fast through small towns, school zones, detours, and red lights, your trip is destined for disaster. (It might make a good movie, though. Let me know if you make it, and I'll consider buying the rights.)

"Speeding" is a no-no game because those who play it try to get from zero to millionaire in the shortest possible time. They invest all (or most) of their money in high-risk, speculative investments with no regard for safety. It's possible that some of them will succeed in getting rich quickly, but the odds are against them. Most people who try this strategy crash or find themselves in front of flashing red lights that signal them to pull over and pay a fine (lose most or all of their money).

Successfully driving across the country (or to a comfortable retirement) takes time if you are going to do it safely and with minimal risk. Speeding (putting all your eggs in one investment basket) is very risky in today's environment of radar and laser speed detection. Police are even using airplanes, unmarked cars, and stopwatches as devices to catch unwary speeders.[37]

It's safest to travel the investment highway by moving at the variety of speeds required by the various road conditions and posted limits. Speed limits change from place to place and time to time, and your investments need to do the same. To travel at different speeds, your car must have a variety of gears. If you've ever driven a car with a manual transmission, you'll understand what I mean. You can't start out from a stoplight in fifth gear. If your car has multiple gears, you'll always have the right gear for the speed you need to go.

Just as a successful jaunt across the country requires you to travel at different speeds and in different gears at different times, successful investing requires you to have a variety of investments that move at different speeds under different circumstances. In the world of investments, this is called diversification.

---

[37] Don't even think about asking how I know that.

To be diversified means to have a mix of investments. The goal of diversification is to protect your overall portfolio from major shocks. The trick is to diversify enough to sleep well, but not so much that you rob yourself of higher long-term returns.

I saw a poster some years ago captioned, "Justification for Higher Education." It showed a beautiful house on a cliff overlooking the ocean, and in the foreground was a five-car garage filled, as I recall, with a Porsche, a Corvette, a Ferrari, and two more exotic cars I didn't recognize. They looked like lots of fun, but in the investment world, that garage would have represented a poorly diversified portfolio. I would to suggest that you fill four stalls of your five-car investment garage with cars such as these:

- A Volvo (an emergency fund or safe investment);
- A Toyota Camry, said by many to be the best car for holding resale value (something for inflation protection);
- A Chrysler minivan to hold your expanding family (something for growth);
- A hybrid or electric car (something for income).

Most of us should probably leave the fifth investment garage stall empty, but that's the spot where some folks put the exotic or experimental car (any of the more speculative investments).

Here's a chart to help you visualize what I'm suggesting:

| PORTFOLIO TYPE | REASON | TYPE OF CAR |
|---|---|---|
| Safety and liquidity | Emergency fund | Volvo |
| Inflation protection | So you don't lose ground. | Toyota Camry |
| Growth | If you want to grow, this is the one to get. | Minivan |
| Income | Not sexy, but will protect your cash | Hybrid or electric vehicle |
| Speculative | You've lost your mind and are hoping to lose your shirt as well. | Exotic or experimental |

Thus, diversification means that you should have a certain percentage of your money in stock and stock funds and a certain amount in bonds, money markets funds, and fixed income funds. Then (as you are able to) within the stock and fixed income categories, you can spread your risk even further. For example, on the stock side, you can split that money into 20 percent aggressive growth, 20 percent growth, 20 percent balanced funds, 20 percent value funds, and 20 percent international funds. The fixed income portion can also be split, perhaps between high-yield bonds, treasury bills, corporate notes, corporate bonds, etc.

Right now you may not know what half of these investments are, let alone have enough cash to invest in even one of them. That's okay. The main thing to remember as you start accumulating your fortune is to spread out your risk along the way.

Investing can be like a roller coaster. It's not uncommon to see several-hundred-point swings in the stock market on a daily basis. It is also not uncommon to see 5–10 percent declines over a period of days. Believe me, when those roller-coaster drops occur, you'll be glad to know that some of your investments (fixed annuities, money market funds, CDs, credit union accounts, etc.) are always going up. They may be slow growers, but they only go one direction!

Why wait until the stock market decides to play like a submarine and dive, dive, dive before you take action and diversify your investments? Better to have a little less income now and better protection in the event that market forces move in contrary directions.

## ACTION STEPS

1. Understand that diversification is the most advanced topic in this book. "Speeding," or putting all your money in one high-risk place, is what you want to avoid.

2. It isn't necessary for you to fully understand the wide variety of investments right now. What is important is that you understand this one basic concept: As you start accumulating money, it is safer to stash parts of it in different investments than to have it all in one place.

3. Spend at least fifteen minutes per day reading about and learning about investments. As you can see from this brief overview, there is much to learn. Be wise and start your learning *before* you've accumulated the cash.

4. Find a trusted advisor. (My definition: Someone who spends 80 percent of the time asking you questions rather than 80 percent of the time pushing his or her own agenda and own investment choices.)

Many advisors won't even talk to you if you have less than $50,000 or $100,000 to invest. However, there are some of us who don't care if you are starting with $50. Our goal is to educate you and to help you build your financial pyramid from the ground up. Look for us.

# The "Albuquerque Low"

## A long, unexpected drive at midnight was the consequence of our failure to plan.

The real Albuquerque low is a weather term that means that low barometric pressure has set up over Albuquerque, New Mexico and that intense weather is likely headed for areas farther north, such as Colorado. In this no-no game, however, I'm going to tell you about an entirely different "Albuquerque low." It has to do with planning and goals—or rather, the failure to have specific goals and the accompanying failure to do any specific planning.

As you know by now, planning and goal-setting are to investing and wealth-creation what road maps and itineraries are to travel. You need to know where you are going and what the stops are along the way if you want to have a successful trip.

I still remember one trip I took from Arizona to Colorado with a friend. We decided when to leave at the last moment and just started driving. Late in the day, we finally looked at our map to figure out a final destination for our first day. It was a stretch, but we figured we could roll into Albuquerque around midnight. Roll in we did ... only to roll right back out again and on to the next big city, which was several *more* hours away.

What happened? Well, if you know about Albuquerque, you'll know that it is the site of the national hot air balloon races. Guess what? They were being held the exact weekend we went through, and every hotel in town was full. A little better advance planning sure would have saved us some grief. A long, unexpected drive at midnight was the consequence of our failure to plan.

Take note that your present financial activities such as planning and goal-setting, whether positive or negative, will also lead to future consequences: rewards or regrets. In light of that, why don't more people take the time to plan their financial futures? Why do so many people practice the no-no version and take actions without regard for their future consequences? Here's my opinion: People are so caught up in the current moment's activities that it just doesn't seem to matter.

If you are not happy with the current state of your financial affairs, the place to start is with your thought process. If you can see in your mind the results you wish to achieve, you will begin taking steps in a positive direction toward those results.

In short, you will have contacted the right travel agent for your dream financial destination.

## ACTION STEPS

1. If you are going to Albuquerque, plan ahead and make sure you don't arrive sans hotel reservations in the event that it's the weekend of the balloon races.

2. If you are not happy with the current state of your financial affairs, avoid encountering the "Albuquerque low."

   • Set goals.

   • Plan ahead.

   • Visualize exactly what you want to achieve and the exact time period in which you want to achieve it. "Make your reservations" in advance!

# The Sin of the Desert

**Truly wealthy people are generally the most giving, sharing, and open people you will ever meet.**

Wow—this is a game with *sin* involved? No wonder this is a no-no game. What in the world is "the sin of the desert?" I read the answer in a quote from Richard Paul Evans: "The sin of the desert is knowing where the water is and not telling anyone." (Evans 2005)

You've heard the well-worn phrase "What goes around comes around," right? The sin of the desert is based on the same principle. If you want to have friends, you have to *be* a friend. If you want to be loved, you must *give* love. If you want to become wiser in the ways of money, you must find someone with whom you can share your knowledge!

Take some time to think through the things you've learned and practiced that have led you to greater wealth. Think through your mistakes and what you learned from them. Now find a willing student and share your wisdom. As in the "Garden Hose" game, sharing knowledge and wisdom works the same way as sharing your possessions; the more you give, the more will come back to you. No matter how dire your personal financial straits are, there will always be someone who has it worse than you do. In fact, there will be many of those people. Find them and share with them. You may share your time, your money, or your knowledge. *What* you share isn't the important thing. The fact that you *do* share is what matters.

Do most of the people you know voluntarily share ideas with you that will help you gain greater wealth and abundance? That certainly hasn't been my experience. I wonder why that is. Is it because people just appear to be wealthy on the outside with their big homes and fancy cars while in reality, they are in debt up to their eyeballs? Is it because it makes them feel important to be wealthier and more knowledgeable than you are? That's also possible. On the other hand, maybe they are just caught up in the sin of the desert. They know where the water is, but they refuse to tell anyone else. (Sounds like a no-no game to me!)

Truly wealthy people, whether they are wealthy in material possessions, wisdom, or both, are generally the most giving, sharing, and open people you will ever meet. Why? They've conquered the sin of the desert. They know where the water is, and they will gladly point you toward the well.

Will you continue "sinning?" By now, you have been exposed to a great many ideas and new ways of interacting with the money in your world. You have the tools that will help you build a more prosperous life if you choose to use them.

*Why not share?*

## ACTION STEPS

1.  Take time to reflect on what you've learned. In the prehistoric era (that is, the time before you read this book), you lived in the desert and had very little water. Now you have learned to irrigate and to build dams, and your water supply is growing!

2.  Make a list of the reasons for your new success. Record your old habits (the ones you've discontinued) on the left-hand side of the page and the new habits you have started on the right side.

3.  How many people can you find who would like to know how to build their own oases in the middle of the financial desert? Offer to share your new knowledge with anyone who is interested. As you share, you will find your own finances improving even more! Giving opens the door for greater abundance to come into your life.

# Yacht-Sea

## First you have to have somewhere to keep the darn thing.

Many of your neighbors play "Yacht-sea," also sometimes known as "Boys and Their Toys." (I'm sure there is a female version too; my female friends tell me they also have many toys. Maybe it could be called "Girls and their Pearls.")

Of course *you* would never play this game, but your neighbors sure do. They're the ones with the bumper stickers on their cars proclaiming, "The Person with the Most Toys WINS!" This game is guaranteed to keep your neighbors poor.

Our first example of "Yacht-sea" could be purchasing that forty-foot (or longer) ocean craft. Now, I will admit to always having wanted a yacht. I even did research and found out that a boat doesn't become a yacht—at least according to Webster—until it is forty feet long or longer.

So what's the problem? If you can afford a luxury toy, why not just get it? That may be okay if you really *can* afford it. Let's say you want a shiny, new, plush Carver Motor Yacht. The forty-foot model is the one you want, of course, as it will allow you to use the word "yacht" when you invite your friends aboard.

You do your research (as I did) and find that the price is $270,000. At, say, 8 percent over twenty years, that's a payment of just over $2,258 per month. Wonderfully, it's even tax deductible as a second residence, so in a 33 percent tax bracket, your net, after-tax cost is only $1,625 per month.

After crunching the numbers in the family budget, you decide, "Yes, we can afford an after-tax payment of $1,625 per month." Therefore, you buy the yacht. Congratulations! May I come aboard and drool?

Only then does it start to sink in that $1,625 per month isn't the entire picture. First, you have to have somewhere to keep the darn thing. It's too big to put on a trailer, and it definitely wouldn't fit in your triple garage. (There's too much stuff in there, and the cars are already living on the street.) So now you need to rent a slip in which to keep your yacht. More bucks down the drain.

Oh, and did you mean to actually take it out of the slip and take it somewhere cool? Maybe you'd like to motor it down to Malibu to one of those "drive-in" restaurants where you can park (sorry, "moor") dockside and casually stroll in for a $400 dinner for two. More bucks.

Oh, and did you happen to think about the fuel costs? Diesel fuel isn't cheap anymore, and you have two huge, throbbing engines to feed! More bucks.

219

Oh, and did you consider the ongoing occasional costs? Who's going to clean off those barnacles that are building up on the bottom of your pleasure craft? Certainly it's beneath you (nice pun!) to have to do that. Better hire someone.

Oh, and I'm sure you considered that all that teak will need to be polished up periodically. Get the drift? More bucks. As with many "toys," the initial costs are just the beginning. Many associated costs come with owning toys like yachts.

Maybe I'll finally break down and get that $40,000 chopper. Can you spell "chick magnet?" If so, then you can probably also spell "tune-ups," "leathers," "helmets," and "wireless headsets," right? Can you spell "custom accessories?" Can you spell "chrome"?

Yacht-sea is an expensive game, isn't it? If you are middle-aged or older, don't you wish you could turn back the clock about twenty years, recapture some of that money you spent on toys, and invest it instead? Maybe you can't undo the past, but you can certainly make better decisions in the future. Start today.

## ACTION STEPS

1. Put together a wish list of all the exceptionally expensive toys you'd really like to have. Put each item on a separate page.

2. Under each item, list not only the expected cost of that particular item but also all the possible expenses that may come along with it. Yes, I hear you— "But my five-carat diamond ring doesn't have any other expenses! Except for getting it cleaned, maybe." That could be true, but once you have the ring, wouldn't a diamond bracelet, a diamond necklace, and diamond earrings really help set it off? Trust me, it won't stop with the ring.)

3. Make your purchasing decisions with an informed mind, not on impulse. You may still decide to purchase that toy, but you will consider future expenses in addition to today's.

# THE FINAL GAME!

# The Antithesis Game

## Live life, love everybody, and *spend* your money!

It's been fun spending all this time with you, discovering how to have fun saving money page after page and idea after idea. As the final game, however, we're going to talk about the antithesis of nearly everything we've covered so far.

Have I lost my mind? After all these pages, am I going to tell you to forget everything we've covered so far and just *spend* all your money? You bet. Life's short. You only get to live it once. Why save up all that money?

Well, not exactly. However, I do want to temper what I've said throughout the book with another perspective that might be useful to you. It is true—life is short. We've had friends die in their forties and fifties recently! That's young. We also had a relative die before completing college. That's extra young. You just never know how many days of life you will be blessed with on this incredible planet. What with wars, famines, droughts, earthquakes, tornadoes, terrorists, fires, plagues, HIV, heart attacks, strokes, plane crashes, car crashes, and rogue solar flares, life is fragile.

Indeed, here we are, sitting on this tiny speck of stardust (residual from the big bang), hurtling through space at something like 63,000 miles per hour toward the outer reaches of an ever-expanding universe ... and we're worried about saving money? What's the matter with *that* picture?

While I don't subscribe to the theory of "Live it all for today, for tomorrow you may be toast," I do think we need to temper our frantic attempts to scrimp and save with some balance. One thing my wife and I learned early on in our now-thirty-one-year-old marriage is that everyone needs at least a little money he or she doesn't have to account for. I need some "mine" money—money with which I can do whatever I want without telling anyone what I did with it. If your budget is tight, this amount may be small for now, but do have some amount that is your own to spend as you please. As your income and circumstances improve, you can always increase your "allowance."

Everybody needs balance and equilibrium. This is true for thought processes as well as money. Imagine an apothecary's scale (a balance with a plate or dish on each side that is used to measure precise amounts). One side of the scale might be labeled "spending for today" and the other side "saving for tomorrow." We each need to make our own decisions about how to divide our money between the two sides. The sides don't need to be equal, but we do need to give conscious thought to how much of our money we place in each dish. You might weight one side more heavily while I might put more weight on the other side. Neither of us will be "right." We each just need to know what is right for ourselves.

How can we each make our own best decisions? One way I like is to list all my financial and life wishes, desires, and goals, including both spending and saving goals, and then to prioritize them so that I can give most weight to what really matters to me most.

Here is a fun way to go about deciding on your priorities. First, list all the things you'd like to have, do, or be that relate to money. Second, take the top two items on the list and decide which one matters to you most. Circle that one. Then compare the circled item with the next (or third) item on your list. Again, circle the one with the highest priority. Follow this process all the way down the list until you have your definite, number-one priority. Put that priority on a separate piece of paper and label it "number one." Then go back to the original list (minus the one you've now removed) and repeat the same process over and over until eventually *all* the items have been ranked in priority order and moved to separate lists.

This is a fascinating exercise, and it's one that spouses and family members can each do on his or her own. Once each person is done, you can get a very lively discussion going about how to merge the lists (or allocate time and money separately, perhaps) so that each person has a share of the family's resources to devote to his or her personal priorities. That should keep you busy for a while!

Is that exercise more than you want to tackle? Maybe this will be an easier route for those of you who would describe yourselves as "very intuitive." If physical balance is affected by the inner ear, perhaps mental or financial balance is affected by the inner "hear." Intuition can be a useful guide if you can learn to listen well. I've made some great decisions by trusting my instincts and intuition, and I've made some poor ones by ignoring them. If it works for you, that's wonderful.

The bottom line is that saving money should merely be a way to help you achieve the goals, dreams, and ambitions that are most important to you. Live life, love everybody (okay, almost everybody), and spend money! Just remember and practice one word: balance.

## ACTION STEPS

1. Live life.
2. Love everybody.
3. Spend money, and ...
4. Live in balance.

# Golden Nuggets

After all is said and done, the teacher usually learns more by teaching and preparing to teach than the students gain from the listening. In the process of compiling these many fun things for you to do to save, save, save, I've learned too.

First, writing this book reminded me so very vividly that I'm not perfect either. I continue to be amazed at how many pieces of wisdom I "know" but often forget to practice. I needed to be reminded that:

- poor people spend first and save what's left; rich people save first and spend what's left.
- wise folks avoid using debt to purchase depreciating assets.
- it isn't good to hold onto your wealth and/or possessions too tightly. When you see someone in need, be willing to share.
- there are no easy answers, but there are easy actions.
- getting rich will be *fun*, but that doesn't mean you won't have to work at it.

Now, as a reward for your patience (may we have a drumroll, please?), here are ...

## The Top TEN Financial "Golden Nuggets"

1. Discover your mission.
   - I believe each of us has been put on this planet for a special purpose. If we can find that purpose and develop the unique set of talents and abilities that lets us be passionate about that mission, our financial futures will be enhanced.
2. Set goals.
   - If you don't know your destination, then the best road maps ever produced will be unable to help you get there. Know exactly what you want. Focus intently on your desired outcome.

3. Pyramids are not built overnight.

   • Building your financial "house" is much like building the pyramids must have been. I think it is safe to assume that building the pyramids took many years. It is also safe to assume that the builders encountered many obstacles, but they probably had a "never give up" attitude that let them overcome every problem.

4. Giving has to be part of any successful financial endeavor.

   • I like the 80/20 split. The first 10 percent of your income should go to charity. The second 10 percent should go to savings and investing. The remainder should be your monthly working budget. (If you are deep in debt, consider a 70/30 split, putting the additional up-front 10 percent toward reducing your liabilities.)

5. We must learn to delay gratification.

   • All choices, including financial decisions, have consequences. Carefully consider the long-range results that will come from every short-range action.

6. The truly wise seek the wisdom of many counselors.

   • Read widely, talk to every financially wise person you can find, and consider many points of view before you make big decisions about your hard-earned money.

7. Learn to enjoy the moment.

   • We don't come into this world with any money, and we can't leave with any either. That means that at best, we are merely caretakers of the money in our lives while we are on earth. A focus on money is okay; an obsession with it isn't. Enjoy life along the way.

8. Consider carefully how you use your time, especially your discretionary time.

   • Twenty-four hours seems to be the average amount of time we each get per day. How are you using yours? If you want to improve your financial situation, you need to spend some of your free time on self-improvement. (Reading this book was a good start. Congratulations!)

9. Spend time serving others.

   • What goes around comes around. What you give, you will receive. Be generous with your time and your money, and abundance will be yours in return.

10. Live with style.

- Love. Give. Live your life in ways that will cause others to truly admire you and your actions.

May God bless you abundantly, and may you share what you've been so richly given. Share from your wealth of money. Share from your wealth of wisdom. Enrich others so that the circle of blessings may continue into eternity.

Randy Petrick

# *References*

(For selected reviews and information on purchasing these and other books related to abundance, please visit *www.wordsofabundance.com*.)

Andrew, Douglas R. *Missed Fortune: Dispel the Money Myth-Conceptions—Isn't It Time You Became Wealthy?* New York: Business Plus, 2004.

Andrew, Douglas R. *The Last Chance Millionaire: It's Not Too Late to Become Wealthy.* New York: Business Plus, 2007.

Brooks, Yvonne. *Daily Financial Journal: Spiritual Leadership Series Volume Two.* New York: iUniverse, Inc., 2006.

Burkett, Larry. *Debt-Free Living.* Chicago: Moody Publishers, 2001.

Carlson, Charles B. *The Individual Investor Revolution: Seize Your New Powers of Investing & Make More Money in the Market.* Columbus: McGraw-Hill, 2000.

Carroll, Ted. *Live Debt-Free: How to Quickly Pay Off Your Credit Cards, Personal Loans, and Mortgages, and Build Real Wealth Today!* Ohio: Adams Media Corporation, 2003.

Clason, George. *The Richest Man in Babylon: Now Revised and Updated for the 21st Century.* New York: Signet, 2004.

Dominguez, Joe and Vicki Robin. *Your Money or Your Life: Transforming Your Relationship with Money and Achieving Financial Independence.* New York: Penguin, 1999.

Evans, Richard Paul. *The Five Lessons a Millionaire Taught Me About Life and Wealth.* New York: Fireside Press, 2005.

Gorchoff, Louis R. *The Directory of Money-Saving Coupons, 2004 Edition: Where to Find Coupons for Groceries and Everything Else You Buy (With Starter Grocery Coupon Certificate Book).* Financial Data Research, LLC., 2004.

Johnson, Stacy. *Life or Debt: A One-Week Plan for a Lifetime of Financial Freedom.* New York: Ballantine Books, 2005.

Kay, Ellie. *Shop, Save, and Share.* Grand Rapids: Bethany House, 2004.

Kingma, Daphne Rose and Dawna Markova. *Random Acts of Kindness.* Newburyport: Conari Press, 2002.

Kiyosaki, Robert. *Rich Dad, Poor Dad.* New York: Time Warner Paperbacks, 2002.

Murray, Nick. *Simple Wealth, Inevitable Wealth.* New York: The Nick Murray Company, 2004.

Orman, Suze. *The 9 Steps to Financial Freedom: Practical and Spiritual Steps So You Can Stop Worrying.* New York: Three Rivers Press, 2006.

Proctor, Bob. *You Were Born Rich: Now You Can Discover and Develop Those Riches.* Scottsdale: Life Success Productions, 1997.

Ramsey, Dave. *Financial Peace Revisited.* New York: Viking Adult, 2003.

Renier, Leonard A. *Learning to Avoid Unintended Consequences.* West Conshohocken: Infinity Publishing, 2003.

Stanley, Thomas J. *The Millionaire Next Door.* Atlanta: Longstreet Press, 1996.

Stav, Julie. *The Money in You!: Discover Your Financial Personality and Live the Millionaire's Life.* New York: Collins, 2007.

Wattles, Wallace D. *The Science of Getting Rich: The Proven Mental Program to a Life of Wealth.* New York: Tarcher, 2007.